CENTRAL STATION

CENTRAL STATION

Screenplay by João Emanuel Carneiro and Marcos Bernstein
(Based on an original idea by Walter Salles)
Translation by John Gledson
Introduction by Walter Salles

BLOOMSBURY

First published in Brasil 1998 as *Central do Brasil*
by Editora Objetiva Ltda., Rio de Janeiro

This edition published 1999

Copyright © 1998, Walter Salles,
João Emanuel Carneiro and Marcos Bernstein

Introduction copyright © Walter Salles 1999
Introduction translation copyright © Garry Trudgian 1999
Screenplay translation copyright © John Gledson 1999

The moral right of the authors and translators has been asserted

Bloomsbury Publishing Plc, 38 Soho Square, London W1V 5DF

A CIP catalogue record for this book
is available from the British Library

ISBN 0 7475 4502 2

10 9 8 7 6 5 4 3 2 1

Drawings by Carla Caffé (text pages 41, 66, 68, 70 and 114)
Photographs by
Ricardo Sá text pages x, 8, 14, 17, 23, 28, 36, 39 and 89;
plate section page 1
Walter Salles text pages 46, 62, 73, 75, 94 (*bottom*) and 99;
plate section pages 4, 5, 6, 7 and 8 (*top*)
Walter Carvalho text pages 61, 80, 94 (*top*) and 106;
plate section page 8 (*bottom*)
Paula Prandini text pages 68, 79, 87 and 109;
plate section pages 2 and 3

Typeset by Hewer Text Ltd, Edinburgh
Printed in Great Britain by St Edmundsbury Press, Suffolk

Introduction by Walter Salles

Five years ago, a sculptor friend of mine, Frans Krajcberg, showed me a letter which had been sent from prison by a woman who had been sentenced to thirty-six years' confinement. Although she was only partially literate, her letter moved us both for its extraordinary sensitivity and shrewdness. She also had the most extraordinary name – 'Socorro Nobre' – which, literally translated, means 'Noble Help'. Socorro's letter told Krajcberg that she had come across his work in an old magazine and how much she had been touched by his art. It should be mentioned here that Krajcberg only works with burnt wood which he salvages from the Amazon region and into which he breathes new life and form. Eventually, I made a documentary on the correspondence between Krajcberg and Socorro. I was most impressed how something so apparently anachronistic as a letter, on the verge of the new millennium with its cold-hearted forms of communication, could change people's lives.

And this was the starting-point for *Central Station*. Out of the documentary arose the idea of making a film about the importance of sending letters that had been stowed away at the back of drawers, a film that would talk of the culture of cynicism and indifference of the last few decades, but that, following Krajcberg's aesthetic and ethical gesture, might bring to the fore the possibility of a different future.

First, it was Dora that came to mind, thick-skinned and world-weary and unmindful of others. Then it was her counterpart in the innocent eyes of Josué, the little boy who rejects the destiny of an abandoned child and grants himself another chance.

Above all, the film attempts to assume the function of a sounding-board of what is said in and by the core of an immense and very real state of affairs – what does not reach the TV channels, what springs from the desire to transcribe one by one hitherto unheard voices. Dora does so, unaware of what she is accomplishing. Through her hands passes a Brazil at the margin of official statistics. But instead of giving voice to her characters and expounding the secular unsaid, Dora does exactly the opposite. She frequently tears up the letters, thereby denying those who rarely, if ever, express the chance to assert their identities.

The film then moves from the polyphony of the station to individual voices, not only those of the main characters, but also those who dictate letters to relatives, or to the saints of Bom Jesus. It is interesting to notice that Dora only manages to settle her debts with the past after putting all the letters in the mail. In this respect, these letters are of more importance than the first ones at the outset of the film.

Claustrophobia versus the open space: the hubs of the development of the script – and the film:

Central Station begins at the largest railroad station in Rio de Janeiro, only, in the second 'movement', to set off on the road towards the Brazilian North-East, an initiatory journey that, little by little, veers towards the centre of the country.

The first part of the film, in the city, was intended to convey a feeling of claustrophobia. The statements are made while the constant to-and-fro of the crowds in the station carries on behind, unfeeling and inexorable. The façades of the external locations, such as the residences of Dora, Irene and Yolanda, are mere extensions of the same world, which gives a feeling of *huis clos* at the beginning of the film. It is as if Dora has no way of escaping from this vicious circle, or as if Josué could never survive it. Visual rhymes, such as the railroad car/corridor in Dora's building and the outside of the train/building of Yolanda, reinforce this impression. There are no horizons in this world, nor skies. Only the constant presence of concrete.

This part of the film verges on monochrome but, when on the road, the film slowly opens up, reveals horizons and explores new colours. It is as if a new geography invades Dora's world which, up to that point, had only known the drab monochrome of the station. The transition between one world and another is aided by the ochre hues of the drought-stricken land of the North-East. Through a careful choice of lenses and the introduction of the new colours, it is intended to give the impression that Dora is beginning to be mindful of others. Face to face with the unknown, Dora has no further control over people's destinies, as she did when she did not send letters. Gradually, she begins to be transformed by this new world and by the characters she meets on the way. For Josué, the journey is even more emblematic. It is the return to a land which he has never seen, the return to an Ithaca unknown to him, but which has dwelled in his imagination.

Meanwhile, the treatment of sound accompanies the same rationale as the images. From the cacophony of the station and the roar of the city that is omnipresent in the homes of Dora, Irene and Yolanda, sounds go through a process in which they gradually become more individualized and rarified as they move farther inland. That is to say, sounds become more easily perceived as Josué grows closer to his family and begins to recover his lost identity, or just as Dora begins to recover her sensitivity.

Some acknowledgments:
Central Station was written by two young scriptwriters, João Emanuel Carneiro and Marcos Bernstein, and is their first full-length movie. It was their talent and insight, which they amply supplied during the two years of hard work, that gave form, density and life to the story-line I had proposed to them.

In January 1996, the script of *Central Station* won the Cinema 100 Award that the Sundance Institute and NHK created to celebrate 100 years of the Lumière's invention. Thanks to the Sundance Institute, we received the excellent creative collaboration of two great scriptwriters, Frank Pierson and Joan Tewkesbury, authors, respectively, of such classics as *Dog Day Afternoon* and *Nashville*. The creative input of producers of the film, such as Arthur Cohn, Lillian Birnbaum and Paulo Brito, has also been a constant. Cinema is, first and foremost, a form of collective expression and *Central Station* would never have come to be were it not for the generosity of all the above mentioned people and of many, many others.

Walter Salles, April 1999

1. VARIOUS SCENES: RIO DE JANEIRO CENTRAL STATION. INT. DAY

A voice echoes from a distant tannoy. Whistles and noises of trains. A forty-year-old woman, with an oval face and heavy make-up, hesitates before she begins to speak.

WOMAN: My love, my heart belongs to you. It doesn't matter what you are or what you've done, I still love you. I love you. All those years you're going to stay locked up in there, I'll stay shut up out here, waiting for you . . .

Trains empty hundreds of people on to the station platforms. On screen, a seventy-year-old man.

MAN: It was a guy that cheated me and I want to send him a letter. Zé Amaro, thanks a lot for what you did to me. I trusted in you and you cheated me. You even ran off with my apartment key . . .

A hand writes what's being said, in refined handwriting, on letter paper. More whistles. The tannoy in the distance announces train arrivals and departures. The hand goes on scrawling on the sheets.

On screen, a woman in her early thirties, a working-class look and a strong North-Eastern accent.[1]

WOMAN: Jesus, you were the worst thing that ever happened to me. I'm not writing to you to say sorry for anything. I'm only writing because your son Josué asked me to. I've told him you're a good-for-nothing, but still and all the lad's got it in his head he wants to know you . . .

JOSUÉ, *a boy some nine years old, looks at her disapprovingly. He's carrying a small knapsack on his back. Finally, the person doing the writing appears:*
DORA, *a woman more than fifty years old, sitting at a little portable table. Her ill-humour, just under the surface, the rather unkempt hair, and the clothes she uses, untidy, almost masculine, make it plain that* DORA *has no interest in making herself attractive.*

DORA: Address . . .

WOMAN: Jesus de Paiva, Volta da Pedra Farm, Bom Jesus do Norte, Pernambuco.

ANA *leaves listlessly with her son, who pulls her by the hand. A young man is now dictating to* DORA.

YOUNG MAN: Hey, sexy . . .

DORA: Sexy?

YOUNG MAN: Feeling your body next to mine, our bodies uniting on that motel bed, our sweat mixing. I still feel, I feel, I . . .

DORA: Intoxicated.

YOUNG MAN: That's it, intoxicated!

A detail of DORA's *hand, who goes on filling the lines of the letters with her careful handwriting. A girl from the country is in front of her.*
GIRL: I can't tell you how to put the address . . .
DORA: No good without the address!
GIRL: Put this down: third house past the baker's, Mimoso, Pernambuco.
One face after another comes on screen.
YOUNG MAN: Cansanção, Bahia.
OLD WOMAN: Carangola, Minas Gerais.
GIRL: District of Relutaba, Ceará.
OLD MAN: Muzambinho, Minas Gerais.
The voices of the people are superimposed on one another until they form a general buzz, which melts into the noise of the crowd. We hear the noise of whistles, of the tannoy announcing train departures, of the screech of wheels on the tracks. DORA's *clock strikes five. She begins to dismantle her little table. A fattish man, with a policeman's look about him, comes over, finishes dismantling the table, and puts it into a corner.* DORA *takes some notes out of her wallet and gives them to the man, whose name is* PEDRÃO.
PEDRÃO: Dona Dora.
DORA: OK?
She gives him some money.
PEDRÃO: Fine. See you tomorrow, Dona Dora.
DORA: See you.
While the credits roll, we accompany DORA *through the labyrinth of shacks where she has her stall. A real circus*

improvised in the imposing railway station of the Central do Brasil, in Rio de Janeiro, where street pedlars and all kinds of odd-job merchants live off selling this and that to the equally poor people on their way to the train. PEDRÃO *chases away a group of street kids who were making a racket.* DORA *follows the flow of the suburban swarm that comes out on to the station platforms. People jump in through the carriage windows to get a seat. She manages to get into a carriage.*

2. CARRIAGE. INT. EARLY EVENING
DORA *is squeezed by the small crowd squashed into the carriage. She manages to hold on to a metal handle, as the train rocks back and forth, screeches along the track and slowly leaves.*

3. AN APARTMENT BLOCK. EXT. EARLY EVENING
Slowly, DORA *goes towards the lower-middle-class apartment block where she lives in the suburbs, weighed down with a bag of shopping.*

4. DORA'S APARTMENT. INT. EARLY EVENING
DORA *opens the apartment door, goes in and goes to the window.*

5. APARTMENT BLOCK. EXT. EARLY EVENING
DORA *is leaning out of the window of her apartment, on the floor above* IRENE'S.
DORA (*off*): Irene! Irene!

IRENE *leans out of her own window.*
IRENE: What?
DORA: Come up here, come now!
IRENE: Coming.
IRENE *obeys* DORA, *as she's getting herself ready.*

6. DORA'S APARTMENT. INT. NIGHT
Later. DORA *croons as she's finishing washing the dishes. In the living-room,* IRENE *tries to get the rickety television to work properly. Irritated, she slaps the TV, which, for a few fleeting moments, manages to pick up a signal.*
IRENE: This piece of crap is as old as me, eh, Dora . . .
DORA *ignores* IRENE'S *comment. She comes into the room crooning, while she takes her apron off.*
DORA: 'The moment's come, the moment's here . . .' Sit here, Irene.
DORA *stops singing her song and smiles mischievously at* IRENE.
DORA (*crooning happily*): 'The time is right, the samba's begun . . .'
DORA *rummages in a bag by her side. She pulls out a handful of the letters she writes in the station.*
IRENE: There you're off again . . . I want to make it quite clear that I'm against this, OK?
DORA *examines the letters, opens one and begins to read.*
DORA (*interrupting her*): 'Joana, my love . . .'

IRENE: Dora . . .

DORA: This is better than a soap. As you say, if we only had a decent TV . . . (*She goes on reading*) 'A call from you is the thing that would make me happiest in this world. Yours, always yours, Cícero.' Sorry, Cícero, that phone's not going to ring.

DORA *makes to tear the letter.*

IRENE: Dora! Dora!

DORA: Take that one.

DORA *puts the letter back in the bag and takes another one out, which she gives to* IRENE. *Excited,* IRENE *starts reading.*

IRENE: 'I saw your ad in the classified section and really, your description was the only one that I liked.'

DORA: That wretch made me write that letter to ten different women . . .

IRENE: 'I'm tall, hazel eyes, smooth hair (DORA *makes it plain his hair is anything but smooth*) and I've been through high-school. They say I'm good-looking.'

DORA: He's as ugly as sin.

IRENE: And the high-school education? He doesn't even know how to write!

DORA: Bin it?

IRENE: Bin it.

IRENE *gives the letter to* DORA, *who tears it up.* IRENE *takes another one from the pile.*

IRENE: 'Jesus, you were the worst thing that ever happened to me . . . see if you can't come and meet your son, who's got it in his head he wants to know you . . .'

DORA: She says the boy wants to know his father, a drunkard. It's her that wants her man back.

DORA *goes to tear the letter up.*

IRENE: Don't tear that one up.

DORA: Why shouldn't I?

IRENE: A child who wants to meet his father, get the family back together!

DORA: So?

IRENE: So. You're going to destroy that!

DORA: The man's a drunkard. He used to beat her up.

IRENE: Yes, but the boy? Is he going to be brought up without a father?

DORA: Better than living with a drunkard who'll beat him up too. That's that: straight in the bin.

IRENE: Hey there, Dora. It's the customer's first letter . . .

DORA (*taking pleasure in this*): Exception!

DORA *makes again to tear the letter.* IRENE *tries to get the letter out of her hand.*

IRENE: Enough of this madness, Dora. I've had enough. I'm off.

DORA: She'll get a lot of punches in that face of hers.

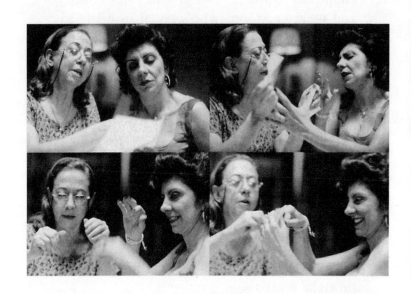

IRENE: So what? It's her face. You haven't got the right . . .
DORA: All right, that letter can go in the drawer.
IRENE: No, no, not the drawer. You're going to put that letter in the mail tomorrow.
DORA: I'm either tearing it up, or it's the drawer. If we decide yes, next week I'll put it in the mail.
IRENE: That's a lie. Those letters stay for years in that purgatory . . .

DORA *stretches out her hand and opens a drawer in the dresser beside her. It's full of letters. She puts the letter in question on to the pile and shuts the drawer.*

DORA: Next week, I'll put it in the mail. Sit down, sit down, love. Let's get to work.
IRENE: Sometimes you're a pain, you know that?

DORA *takes another letter from the pile and begins to read it.*

DORA: 'They say lots of people lose their head at Carnival. I'm one of them. You had a good time and so did I. Now let's forget it.'
IRENE: That's a good one.
DORA: Really? Did you really like it a lot?

DORA *tears the letter.*

7. CENTRAL RAILWAY STATION. EXT. DAY
The crowds get out of the crammed trains and invade the empty platforms.

8. CENTRAL RAILWAY STATION. INT. DAY

DORA *once again gets pencil and paper ready to begin writing. She is listening to a customer, a black gentleman of about fifty.*

CUSTOMER: It's a long time since I had a letter from back home. I don't think they get the letters I send.

DORA: You know you can't trust the lousy mail service. And how about if they've moved?

CUSTOMER: You really think so . . .

DORA: That's 1 *real*,[2] Sérgio.

The man gives an uneasy, cowardly smile, pays up and takes his letter.

SÉRGIO: See you, Dona Dora.

DORA: Ciao.

To DORA'S *displeasure,* ANA *and* JOSUÉ *are in the queue again. Like the first time, the boy is playing with his spinning top, and carrying his little knapsack on his back. Embarrassed,* ANA *comes up to the table.*

ANA (*hesitating*): The other day I sent a letter through you, d'you remember?

DORA: I know.

DORA *gets her paper set, and is ready to write.*

ANA: Did you already put the letter in the mail?

DORA: No, I'm going to mail it today.

ANA: Oh great! Because I want to rip that one up. I wanted to send another. I was too mad at him and . . .

DORA *quickly picks any old letter out of the pile and rips it up.*

DORA: You can start.

ANA *concentrates.*

ANA: Jesus, Josué, your son, really wants to know you . . .

DORA: . . . know you . . .

ANA: . . . and he wants to go to Bom Jesus to spend some times . . .

DORA (*interrupting*): Time.

ANA: . . . some time with you. Next month is my holidays and I can go with him. So I can see Moisés and Isaías too . . .

DORA: . . . and Isaías too . . .

ANA: Oh lady! What I really want is to see that good-for-nothing's face again!

DORA *can't disguise the contempt she feels for this woman.*

ANA (*goes on, pleading*): Lady, you've got experience . . . What can I say to him now?

DORA (*impatient*): How should I know, madam?

ANA: Help me out, lady . . .

DORA: Look, why don't you think it over and come back another day . . .

ANA (*interrupting*): The truth that I still like him a lot, see . . .

With an air of supreme annoyance, DORA *begins to dictate as she writes.*

DORA (*ironic*): Jesus, I miss you a lot. It hurts to

wake up in the morning and not have you by my side.

To DORA'S *utter irritation,* JOSUÉ *plays with the top on her table, disturbing her work pencils.* DORA *pushes the top away with her hand.*

DORA: I'd leave the last black hair on my head for you to take out!

ANA (*moved*): That's it! That's it!

DORA (*beginning to believe in what she's saying*): Wait for me, I'm coming back to you. Your . . . (*To the woman*) what's your name, madam?

ANA: Ana.

DORA *folds the paper.* ANA *opens her bag, takes out a photograph of her son, and gives it to* DORA. *As she takes the photo out of the bag, she leaves her handkerchief on the table.*

ANA: Put this inside the letter.

DORA *puts the little photo inside the letter.*

DORA: There it is, inside the letter. Do you want me to send it or not?

ANA: Yes, you can send it. How much is that?

DORA: 2 *reals*. No, less one for the letter I haven't sent. 1 *real*.

The woman is searching for some coins, when JOSUÉ *pulls her by the hand.*

JOSUÉ: Hey, Mum, how do you know she's going to put it in the mail? She's not even put it in the envelope . . .

DORA *gives the boy a sharp look.*
ANA: Don't be so rude. Can't you see the lady's trying to help your mother?
ANA *leaves the handkerchief on the table and gives* DORA *the money.*
DORA: Next!
ANA: See you.
DORA *watches the two going away and disappearing from view amongst the people waiting to cross the street.*

9. CENTRAL RAILWAY STATION. EXT. DAY

JOSUÉ *throws his top on to the ground. With the street empty,* ANA *and others cross. The top is knocked out of* JOSUÉ'S *hand. In the middle of the asphalt,* ANA *stops and turns round to* JOSUÉ.
ANA: Come on, Josué, come on!
The lights go to stop. ANA *starts walking again. Suddenly, a bus at full speed appears at the corner. The top spins out of its axis.*
JOSUÉ: Hey, my top!
ANA *hesitates, turns round again to the child. A sudden screech of brakes. A foot kicks the top. We watch* JOSUÉ'S *face while we hear shouts and sounds of confusion. Underneath a bus is* ANA'S *body. Paralysed,* JOSUÉ *is thrown far away from his mother's body, in the middle of people elbowing one another out of the way. A small crowd is soon formed. Some, angrier than others, punch the metal sides of the bus. Others shout, accusing the driver.*

VOICES IN THE CROWD (*off*): The light was at red. / Bastard! / Murderer! / Call an ambulance!

10. CENTRAL RAILWAY STATION. INT. DAY
DORA *gets up and tries to see what's happened from her table.* PEDRÃO *comes up to her.*
DORA: What's happened?
PEDRÃO: The bus's driven over a woman.
DORA: Is she dead?
PEDRÃO: She'll be settling her accounts up above by now.
DORA *organises her equipment on the table and notices the handkerchief that* ANA *forgot.*

11. CENTRAL RAILWAY STATION. INT. AFTERNOON
JOSUÉ *is crying, sitting on a bench in the station concourse. Faces of people in the station looking at him.*

12. CENTRAL RAILWAY STATION. INT. AFTERNOON
DORA *checks the money that a customer gives her. To her surprise, she comes upon* JOSUÉ *standing in front of her table.*
CUSTOMER: Many thanks, ma'am.
JOSUÉ: I want to send a letter to my father. Go on, write it: Father, come here to Rio because Mother's hurt herself and . . .
DORA: Have you got money?
JOSUÉ (*fibbing*): Yes.

DORA: Show me. Show me.
JOSUÉ *looks down.*
DORA: Who do you know here in Rio?
JOSUÉ: My mother.
DORA: And who else?
JOSUÉ (*no reply; aggressive*): Go on. Write that letter; I'm telling you to!
DORA: Only if you show me the money.
JOSUÉ: Then give my mother's letter back!
DORA: I've already put it in the mail. Now if you don't mind, son. Clear out . . .
JOSUÉ: Give me my mother's letter back!
DORA: Look, child, clear out! Out of here! Get out of here, kid! Out of here!
An impatient customer is waiting behind JOSUÉ.
CUSTOMER: Come on, clear off, you little brat!
JOSUÉ *gives* DORA *and the customer a look of hatred and moves away.*

13. CENTRAL RAILWAY STATION. EXT./INT. DUSK
DORA *gets into the train, which whistles to signal that it's about to leave. Finally, she sees the static figure of the boy on the platform, opposite the carriage she's in. Another whistle. The doors shut. The train leaves.*
JOSUÉ *impulsively runs after the train.*

14. CENTRAL RAILWAY STATION. INT. NIGHT
The boy wanders round the empty concourse, then kneels in front of a statue of the Virgin and child. The

clock strikes midnight. Apart from him, all you can see in the huge central concourse of the station are some beggars and street children. A guard appears who throws them all out of the station.
GUARD: C'm'on, out! Outa there, you little brat!

15. CENTRAL RAILWAY STATION. INT. NIGHT
JOSUÉ *is sleeping alone under the stairs in a tunnel beneath the station.*

16. CENTRAL RAILWAY STATION. INT./EXT. MORNING
We see the flow of people coming through the tunnels that empty out on to the station platforms.

17. CENTRAL RAILWAY STATION. INT. DAY
The station concourse is filled with the crowd on their way to the trains. PEDRÃO *throws out a group of lads on the look-out for something to rob.*
PEDRÃO: Hey, hey! What's all this? Outa here, out, come on!

18. BAR AND CONCOURSE OF THE CENTRAL RAILWAY STATION. INT. DAY
DORA *is eating a sandwich with some coffee in one of the station bars. She finds* JOSUÉ *sleeping behind one of the pilasters. She goes over to him, bends down and shakes him.*
DORA: Hey, kid, wake up.
JOSUÉ *wakes up to find* DORA *looking at him.*

DORA: Don't you want a sandwich? (*Pause*) Aren't you hungry?
JOSUÉ (*unsmiling*): I've eaten, thank you.
DORA *doesn't argue. She gets up and goes back to the bar. A stall-holder in the station shouts.*

19. CENTRAL RAILWAY STATION. EXT. DAY
In the improvised little stalls in the station, those who've got nothing more to sell show their last possessions: a half-used bottle of perfume, a bar of soap, a wallet for carrying portraits.
STALL-HOLDER: Come on, folks, last chance! Beauty products. 1 *real* for a mirror, 50 cents a comb!

A young girl with an innocent look and a southern accent begins to dictate to DORA.
GIRL: Everything's fine here. I've got more and more customers. I can hardly cope with it all. I'm putting a bit of money together to go back to school, because I'll soon be too old for the work.

Near DORA'S *stall, an eighteen year old grabs a Walkman laid out on one of the stands and runs off. The owner reacts immediately.*
OWNER: My Walkman! Stop, thief! Stop! Stop, thief!
PEDRÃO *waves in the direction of a short fat man, who immediately starts running with him after the lad.*
PEDRÃO: Go on, after him!

20. CENTRAL RAILWAY STATION. INT. DAY
People who don't get out of the way are pushed to one side or on to the floor by the man doing the chasing, who gets closer and closer to the lad. A train whistles for departure. The lad manages to cross through a carriage full of people and jump on to the next platform. The man chasing him also manages to cross through the carriage before the doors shut. Finally he catches up with him.
PURSUER: Shuddup, shut your mouth!
PEDRÃO *calmly comes up to the two men. The thief is on the ground, with the pursuer's gun pointing at him.* PEDRÃO *takes his revolver out. The train leaves, hiding them from view.*
THIEF: Wait, don't kill me, I'll give it back . . .
A gunshot is heard.

21. CENTRAL RAILWAY STATION. INT. DAY
With a chummy air, PEDRÃO *gives the Walkman back to the owner who'd been robbed.* DORA, *with her eye on the man, is paying almost no attention to the customer.*

22. CENTRAL RAILWAY STATION. INT. LATE AFTERNOON
The station clock shows 6 p.m. DORA *is picking up her belongings to finish her day's business. A man, who lives on the Central Line, says goodbye to her.*
MAN: Good-night, Dona Dora!

DORA: Ciao!
MAN: Coming.
He finds PEDRÃO *talking to* JOSUÉ *in a corner.*
PEDRÃO *goes close up to the boy, who is playing with his top. He smiles at him.*
PEDRÃO: Hey, sonny . . .
JOSUÉ: Josué.
PEDRÃO: OK, fine. Let me see this top.
JOSUÉ *silently hands over the top. He's a bit scared. The man spins the top on the ground.*
PEDRÃO: I know what it is. Your mother told you not to talk to strangers. That's right.
The man shows he knows how to play with the toy.
PEDRÃO: Now, you've no need to be afraid of me.
JOSUÉ *faces* PEDRÃO.
JOSUÉ: I'm *not* frightened of you.
PEDRÃO *is surprised to find* DORA *behind him.*
DORA: It's OK, Pedrão. I know the boy.
PEDRÃO: Do you? Then I'd like a little word with you.
The two of them leave JOSUÉ *and go on talking.*
JOSUÉ *observes* PEDRÃO *and* DORA's *conversation. You can't hear what they are saying.*

23. CONCOURSE. INT. AFTERNOON
DORA *sits on a bench by the boy.*
DORA: Hi, sonny.
JOSUÉ: My name is Josué Fontenele de Paiva.

Father's name Paiva, mother's name
Fontenele.

DORA: That's great, terrific! Mine is Isadora
Teixeira. Well then, Josué de Paiva, wouldn't
you like to come home with me?

JOSUÉ: I've already said. I'm waiting for my
mother.

DORA: She's not coming back.

JOSUÉ: That's a lie!

DORA: She's not coming, son, she's dead.

JOSUÉ *looks at her, crushed. She changes tone, sorry for
what she's just said.*

DORA: Have you got any relatives here in Rio?
An aunt or anything?

JOSUÉ *pretends not to have heard the question.*

DORA: Answer me, lad!

JOSUÉ *shakes his head.*

DORA: Then come with me.

JOSUÉ *shows no sign of moving.* DORA *gives a train
ticket to the boy.*

DORA: Look here, take this. If by any chance you
change your mind, all you need to do is
follow me, OK? No sweat.

DORA *carries on walking along the station platform,
looking back from time to time.*

JOSUÉ *follows her with his eyes. He gets up and finally
goes towards her, without much conviction.* DORA *gets
into a full carriage.*

24. DORA'S APARTMENT. INT. NIGHT

DORA *comes in with* JOSUÉ.

DORA: Come on in!

JOSUÉ: Where's your husband?

DORA: I haven't got a husband.

JOSUÉ: And your children?

DORA: No children, no husband, no family, no dog.

JOSUÉ: Can I go to the bathroom then?

DORA: Course you can.

JOSUÉ: Where is it?

DORA: There.

25. LIVING-ROOM. INT. NIGHT

DORA *opens the door for* IRENE, *who comes in breathless, her blouse sweaty under the arms.*

IRENE: Hi, Dora! God, the heat's unbearable! I'm going to the bathroom to wash my face.

IRENE *goes straight to the bathroom. She's surprised to find the door locked from the inside.*

DORA: I've brought a visitor today . . .

IRENE (*ironic*): A visitor?

JOSUÉ *opens the bathroom door and comes face to face with* IRENE.

DORA: This is Josué.

26. DORA'S LIVING-ROOM. INT. NIGHT

DORA *and* IRENE *clear the table. There is an obvious natural sympathy between* JOSUÉ *and* IRENE.

IRENE: Did you enjoy that?

JOSUÉ *doesn't reply.*

DORA: See what a fussy guest I've got, Irene.

IRENE: Don't worry, Dora. His mother's food must have been better.

JOSUÉ: No, she was no good at cooking either.

DORA: Look here, you should be more grateful, kid.

JOSUÉ: Irene, what do you do for a living?

IRENE: Guess?

JOSUÉ: I know, you look like a teacher, just like Dora. Only she's a letter-writer.

IRENE: You're right. We were teachers.

JOSUÉ: And haven't you got a husband either?

IRENE: No, me neither.

JOSUÉ: And who looks after you then?

IRENE: We look after ourselves.

DORA: And didn't your mother live on her own? Who looked after her?

JOSUÉ: Me.

The two women laugh.

IRENE: And what about your father, has he never turned up?

JOSUÉ: He works too much. (*Pause*) He's a carpenter. He works with wood. He knows how to make tables, chairs, doors, tops, houses. All on his own, OK?

IRENE (*to* DORA): Hey, wasn't he . . . ?

DORA *looks at* IRENE, *not too pleased.* IRENE *gets the message.*

DORA: And you? What do you want to do when you grow up?

JOSUÉ: I'm going to be a truck-driver.

IRENE: My father and hers drove those enormous trains, you know.

DORA (*interrupting*): And they were a pair of old soaks too. A pile of shit.

27. DORA'S APARTMENT. INT. NIGHT

The TV won't work properly. DORA *is in the kitchen finishing the washing-up.* JOSUÉ *stops watching the TV and goes to the window, drawn by the noise of a train.*

DORA (*from the kitchen*): Everything OK there, Josué?

JOSUÉ *examines the things in the room. He stops to look at the image of a simple house, painted on a plate hanging on the wall. He looks at a little picture with the Virgin Mary protecting the Child Jesus. He notices a photo of* DORA *posing with the children in her class. Now he sees that one of the drawers of the chest is part-open, revealing a disordered pile of letters.* JOSUÉ *opens the drawer. Right on top of the pile, he recognises his photo sticking out of his mother's letter to his father. He opens it and takes the photograph.*

DORA *comes into the room to bring bed-linen and catches* JOSUÉ.

DORA: Hey, kid, what're you doing there?!
DORA *sees the letter in the child's hand and blushes.*
DORA: Do you know how to read? (*Continuing*) I know. You're thinking I won't send your mother's letter? No, lad, that's not it at all. I've not stopped for the last few days, and I've not had time to put it in the mail.
JOSUÉ: I'm going to take that letter to my father. Give it here!
DORA: What's that? You crazy?! D'you know where your father lives? He lives thousands of kilometres from here. On another planet, OK?
JOSUÉ: I'm going to take it there.
DORA: You'll never get there. Leave it to me, I'll put it in the mail tomorrow. That's the best way. I swear I will.
JOSUÉ *sits on the sofa and looks at* DORA.
JOSUÉ: D'you promise, you swear?
DORA: I swear, I promise.
JOSUÉ: You won't lie to me again?
DORA: No.

28. DORA'S APARTMENT. INT. NIGHT
In the morning, DORA *wakes up and finds herself still sitting on the armchair, next to* JOSUÉ. *She takes a good look at the sleeping boy before she suddenly gets up.*

29. TRAIN. INT. DAY
DORA *and* JOSUÉ *are sitting on a carriage-seat.*
JOSUÉ: Where are we going to?
DORA: You're going to a great place, OK?

30. RAILWAY LINE. INT./EXT. DAY
The train goes round a curve.

31. APARTMENT BLOCK IN THE SUBURBS. EXT. DAY
We see the curved exterior of a huge and long apartment block in the suburbs. The camera pans and finds DORA *and* JOSUÉ *walking through the pillars under the building. We come on the figure of* PEDRÃO, *leaning on a pillar, impatiently looking at his watch. As soon as* PEDRÃO *notices her, he smiles broadly.*
DORA: Hi, Pedrão.
PEDRÃO: Greetings, Dona Dora. Hi, sonny! We're late already.
DORA *and* JOSUÉ *join* PEDRÃO. JOSUÉ *observes the scene with surprise.* DORA *tries not to look at him. The three of them go in at the entrance to the building.*

32. BUILDING/APARTMENT IN THE SUBURBS. INT. DAY
DORA, PEDRÃO *and* JOSUÉ *get to the door of the apartment.* PEDRÃO *knocks on the door. A middle-aged woman,* YOLANDA, *full of smiles, opens the door.*
YOLANDA: Hi, Pedrão! Hi! Come on in! Hi!
PEDRÃO: Yolanda, this is Dona Dora.
The three go in.

YOLANDA: Nice to meet you, Dora! . . . I don't know what he told you but, as you can see, we treat our children as if they were part of a family.

PEDRÃO: They all go to live with rich families in Europe, in the States. They'll all be loaded with dollars when they grow up. (*To* JOSUÉ) But you won't forget us, will you?

JOSUÉ *stares grimly at* PEDRÃO. *In the living-room, a small child is playing with a toy on the floor. Trying hard to be as nice as possible,* YOLANDA *doesn't stop talking, without taking her eyes off* JOSUÉ. *She comes up to* JOSUÉ *and hugs him. She takes advantage of the proximity to look at him closely.*

YOLANDA (*with a stupid look*): Now show Auntie your tongue.

He hesitates and looks to DORA *for protection.*

DORA: Go on, show it.

YOLANDA: Go on, let him be naughty if he wants. (*She smiles*) Yes! That's great!

Half clumsily, JOSUÉ *does as* YOLANDA *asks.*

DORA: I'd like to know a few more things . . .

PEDRÃO *looks disapprovingly at* DORA.

YOLANDA: Of course. We'll have a talk in a minute. (*To* JOSUÉ) what was your name again?

JOSUÉ *doesn't answer.*

DORA: Josué.

YOLANDA: Well then, Josué? D'you like videogames? How's about a great big ice-cream to go with it?

JOSUÉ: No thanks.

YOLANDA *turns round to the other two.* JOSUÉ *is sitting down and staring at them.*

YOLANDA: Let's go and play over there, with Shirlene . . . (*To Dora*) Look, this is yours. Pedrão told you how much, didn't he?

YOLANDA *gives the money to* PEDRÃO.

PEDRÃO: Two thousand dollars. A thousand for you.

YOLANDA: A thousand.

PEDRÃO *takes his part and gives the rest to* DORA. DORA *counts it.*

PEDRÃO: That's fine.

DORA: Ciao, Josué.

YOLANDA: Goodbye.

DORA: Goodbye.

DORA *and* PEDRÃO *leave the apartment.* YOLANDA, *with even more smiles, shuts the door behind them.*

33. DORA'S APARTMENT BLOCK. EXT. AFTERNOON
DORA *carries an enormous cardboard box through the pillars.*

34. DORA'S APARTMENT. INT. NIGHT
IRENE *is flabbergasted: on* DORA'S *chest of drawers there is now enthroned a spanking new TV with a 20-inch screen. Beside it is the half-open cardboard box.*

IRENE: Holy Mother of God!

DORA (*triumphant*): We've come into the age of remote control!

IRENE: Is it stereo?

DORA *shows her the remote control.*

DORA: Only this piece of crap doesn't work.

IRENE: Oh, maybe the battery's flat. And Josué? How did things go at the court?

DORA: Just fine. He's going to the best institution for children there is out there. I spoke to the judge.

IRENE: What institution's that?

DORA (*she thinks*): The Padre Jesuíno Vidal Foundation in Pelotas, right down there in Rio Grande do Sul.

IRENE: Pelotas . . . I thought he'd stay here, so we could visit him . . .

DORA: That way you'll get to know Pelotas. Aren't you the one that's so keen on travelling? This thing's not working.

IRENE *takes the remote control out of* DORA'S *hand and puts the batteries in.*

IRENE: No, Dora, here. Is he still down at the court? I'd like to visit him.

DORA *sits fascinated with the remote control.*

DORA: No . . . I don't think so. He must've gone to Pelotas already.

IRENE *sits down on the sofa. She begins to have doubts about* DORA. *She looks at the TV and at her.*

IRENE: Where did you get the money from to buy that?
DORA: From a gold ring I sold a while back.
IRENE: You're lying. You'd never give your reasons for anything, unless you were lying.
DORA: All right, Irene, I'm lying and you know everything about me. But, just for now, let's watch television . . .
IRENE: Where did you get the money to buy that, Dora? Tell me the truth, please. *On television appear the words* 'Topa tudo por dinheiro' *(They'll do anything for money).*
DORA (*after a pause, looking serious*): A friend of mine at the station, he knows people who send those children to families abroad.
IRENE: I don't believe you did that!
DORA: It's better for him. Better than staying here and ending up in one of those state orphanages!
IRENE: You don't read the papers, love! That's no adoption, no way! They kill the children to sell their organs!
DORA: It's nothing like that! I was there!
IRENE: He's too grown-up to be adopted, Dora!
DORA: Shut up, Irene, don't be such a pain! Don't let's talk about it any more.
IRENE: There's a limit to everything!
IRENE *goes out, slamming the door.*

35. DORA'S BEDROOM. INT. EARLY MORNING
In bed, DORA tosses and turns, unable to sleep, with the noise of the railway in the background.

36. DORA'S APARTMENT. INT. DAY
It's morning. DORA goes to the living-room and takes a pile of letters out of the chest, which she opens, taking out several photos of children. She takes all the money that was in a little box.

37. BUILDING/APARTMENT IN THE SUBURBS. INT. DAY
The adoption woman opens the door again. She's almost unrecognisable without the smile that seemed stamped on her face.

DORA: Hi. I was here yesterday.

YOLANDA: I know.

DORA: Well, when I got back home, I thought you might be interested in more children.

DORA *hands the woman the envelope with the photographs.*

YOLANDA: I'm sorry, madam, but for the time being we've no need of more children.

DORA: Are you sure? These ones are lovely. Look!

MAN'S VOICE (*off*): Yolanda, who's there?

YOLANDA (*thinks for a moment*): Look, just a minute and I'll go and have a word with my partner.

Determined, DORA *goes into the corridor and stops in front of the first door on the left. Holding her breath, she slowly opens it. It's an empty room, with two cases on the floor. She goes further along the corridor. Another open door. A toilet. At the third door, she finds a dark room. To her relief, she discovers it really is* JOSUÉ. *She tries to wake him.*

DORA (*shaking him*): Josué come on, quick, wake up. Josué, come on, quick, wake up.

She shakes him harder. The boy wakes up, but reacts badly to seeing her.

JOSUÉ: What're you doing here? Go away.

DORA: Come on, let's get out.

JOSUÉ: I'm not going.

DORA: Come with me.

JOSUÉ: Liar! Go away.

DORA: Come with me. Come with me.

JOSUÉ: I'm not going. You're no good.

DORA: Come on, kid!

JOSUÉ: No!

DORA: Don't talk so loud.

She listens to noises in the apartment. She tries to pull the child, but he shouts.

JOSUÉ: Let me go or I'll get Yolanda.

DORA: You're calling no one.

More noises are heard. DORA *pulls* JOSUÉ *by the arm and drags him to the door. The two risk crossing the corridor to the living-room. At this moment, the woman*

appears at the end of the corridor. She comes face to face with DORA *trying to open the door.*

DORA *runs to shut the door between the living-room and the corridor. Finally,* DORA *manages to shut the door.* YOLANDA *beats on the door.*

YOLANDA: What's going on? You bitch! Cow! I'll get you!

DORA *runs to the front door. She's so nervous that she can't unbolt the door. Finally, she manages to open it.*

YOLANDA (*off*): João, João!

JOÃO (*off*): You bitch, you're dead!

The two of them go out of the door and run to the stairs.

YOLANDA (*off*): Whore, bitch! Tart! You cow! I'll get you! I'll kill you! You've had it! You're dead!

38. AVENUE IN THE SUBURBS. EXT. DAY

DORA *tries to hail a taxi, which doesn't stop. She's in a state of shock.*

39. STREET IN THE SUBURBS. EXT. DAY

JOSUÉ *and* DORA *are in a moving taxi.* DORA *speaks to the driver.*

DORA: Esperanto Street, Cascadura.

DORA *is in a cold sweat. She takes* JOSUÉ'S *mother's handkerchief out of her bag. Nervously, she wipes her forehead and* JOSUÉ'S. *He pushes her away. She looks out of the back window, tense.*

DORA: Driver, I've changed my mind.

40/41. TELEPHONE BOOTH/IRENE'S APARTMENT.
INT. AFTERNOON

IRENE *answers the telephone, breathless.*

DORA *is in a telephone booth. It's a terrible line.*

> (*Cuts from one to the other*)

DORA: Hello, Irene?

IRENE: Yes?

DORA: Irene.

IRENE: Who is it?

DORA: Guess.

IRENE: Oh, it's a good thing you called . . .

DORA: Irene, pay attention to me! If a guy turns up there, a bulky guy with a moustache, asking if I'm anywhere in the building, just play dumb, right, don't go out of your way, don't invite him in for coffee, OK?

IRENE (*flustered*): Well, um . . .

DORA: I don't believe it . . .

IRENE: Uh-huh . . .

DORA: He's there already? (*Pause*) If he is, say any old thing to put him off . . . *Behind* IRENE, *the shapeless figure of* PEDRÃO *can be seen spread out on the sofa.*

IRENE (*changing her tone of voice*): Milton, I can't go out with you today because I've already fixed to go out dancing with another friend of mine . . .

DORA: No, I'm not saying any more.

IRENE: Where are you, Milton, at the barracks?

DORA: I'm at the bus station. I'm done for.

IRENE: And that friend of yours, the youngster, is he on duty with you?

DORA: Josué's here with me. I ran away with him . . .

IRENE (*holding back her emotion*): I always said you were a good soldier!

DORA: Irene, I'm going to ask you a favour, see . . . You lock up my apartment, with all the keys, you hear? With all the keys! And you be very careful too. I want to ask you another favour.

IRENE: Go on.

DORA: Lend me 200 *reals* and send it to the Banco do Brasil in Bom Jesus do Norte, I think I'm going to need it . . .

42. BUS STATION. INT. NIGHT

DORA *comes up to the boy and holds out a bus ticket.*

DORA: Here, take your ticket. It's almost time!

JOSUÉ *doesn't move.* DORA *walks up to him.*

DORA: Come on, kid, take it!

JOSUÉ *doesn't react.*

DORA (*cont.*): Don't you see I'm trying to help you?

JOSUÉ *takes the ticket from* DORA's *hand.*

JOSUÉ: I'm going on my own.

DORA: I've already said I'm going with you.

JOSUÉ: I don't want to go with you.

DORA: And why not?

ON THE ROAD

RODOVIARIA RIO - telefone - motorista - onibus

JOSUÉ: Because I don't like you.
DORA (*upset*): And why not?
JOSUÉ: I've told you already. You're no good.
DORA: How are you going to get there, can you tell me that?
JOSUÉ: Leave me a bit of money so I can get something to eat.
Another silence.
JOSUÉ: When I get there, my father'll send you money.
DORA (*shocked*): Idiot!
JOSUÉ: Give me my mum's letter.
DORA *takes the letter out and holds it out to the boy, a bit hesitantly. He puts it in his pocket, gets up, adjusts his knapsack and goes off towards the bus-departure platform, right opposite where they are.* DORA *sits watching the boy cross the concourse and go on to the platform. The driver starts the bus and calls the last people who are still on the platform saying goodbye to their relatives. The last passengers get on.* DORA *gets up and goes towards the platform. The driver shuts the door. The bus begins to move. At the last moment,* DORA *runs, bangs on the bus door and makes it stop.*

43. BUS. INT. NIGHT
DORA *gets on to the bus and sits down by* JOSUÉ'S *side as if she didn't know him. She lowers the seat-arm to mark out her territory.*

44. BUS. INT. NIGHT
Through the window, you can see the last lights of Rio and the airport lights. DORA *is very tired, and her eyes are almost closing.* JOSUÉ *looks at her with curiosity.*

45. FIRST STOP. EXT. DAWN
The bus stops at a service-station by the edge of the road. DORA *and* JOSUÉ *walk towards the toilets.* DORA *notices nearby a small pedlar's stall with clothes for sale. She changes tack and goes that way.* JOSUÉ *is soon interesting himself in shirts with collars and long terylene trousers.*
DORA: What do you want that shirt for? Going to get married?
JOSUÉ (*serious*): It's for when I meet my father.

46. FIRST STOP. INT. DAYLIGHT
DORA *and* JOSUÉ *reappear at the doors to the toilet, wearing their new clothes.*
DORA: What're you looking at, kid? Get on the bus, I'm going to buy something. Go on.

47. ON THE ROAD. EXT. DAY
North of Minas Gerais. The landscape on either side of the road is already very dry.

48. BUS. INT./EXT. DAY
The heat is unbearable.
JOSUÉ: Is it still a long way?

DORA: What's a long way?
JOSUÉ: My father's house.
DORA: Keep looking at the signs along the road, you'll see how far there is to go.
JOSUÉ *counts the signs measuring the kilometres.*
JOSUÉ: How do they count a kilometre?
DORA: A kilometre's a kilometre, that's a thousand metres.
JOSUÉ: I know, but how do they know there really are a thousand? How do they count them?
DORA: They make it up.
The bus is shaken by the pot-holed road. DORA *takes a bottle of cheap wine out of her bag and begins to drink.*

49. BUS. INT. LATE AFTERNOON
DORA *has already drunk more than half the bottle. She spills a little of the wine on her clothes.* JOSUÉ *is looking at the men on the bus.*
JOSUÉ: D'you think that guy there's a father?
DORA: What's that?
JOSUÉ: That guy there with a beard. D'you think he's got a son?
DORA *looks at the man.*
DORA: No, that one doesn't look like a father.
DORA *points to another man, who's smiling, and seems to be telling jokes.*
DORA (*cont.*): That one looks like a father. I know the type. My father was like that. At home,

all prim and proper. Outside, he was a clown. One day, they asked me: 'Are you old Willy's daughter?', that was his nickname, Willy, just think: 'Hey, Willy!' . . . a clown, he was a clown.

JOSUÉ *is impatient, and can't sit still on the seat.*

JOSUÉ: I don't like buses. What's really good is going in a taxi.

DORA: That's not so! We should always go by bus, never in taxis. The bus always knows where it's going, it's on the right road . . . But the taxi isn't. It takes any old road and then gets lost.

JOSUÉ: Why?

DORA: All that was in a letter my father sent my mother. All that to say that he was tired of going by bus every day – meaning my mother – so he decided to get a taxi, that is, another woman . . .

DORA *looks serious.*

DORA (*cont.*): It was my mother took a taxi into space. I was your age when she died.

JOSUÉ *looks at her with curiosity*: DORA *takes a swig from the bottle.*

50. THE ROAD. EXT. DUSK
The bus journeys on.

51. BUS. INT. NIGHT
DORA *sleeps.* JOSUÉ *takes several swigs from the bottle of wine.*

52. BUS. INT. NIGHT
DORA *is woken by the shouts of a passenger. She tries to find out what the fuss is about. She catches sight of* JOSUÉ *sitting on the corridor floor. With the start of the confusion, a woman wakes up.*
WOMAN (*shouting*): Get back to your seat, lad!
JOSUÉ: Josué Fontenele de Paiva! I'm Josué Fontenele de Paiva! OK!
PASSENGER: Hey, look, folks! The youngster's had a skinful!
DORA *jumps up and runs towards* JOSUÉ. *She helps him get up.*
OLD WOMAN: You're crazy! Giving drink to a child like that!
DORA: You just stick to your own affairs! (To JOSUÉ) Shit! If I was your mother I'd not half clobber you . . .
JOSUÉ (*rolling his tongue around a bit*): But you're not my mother. You're nothing to do with me!
DORA: You'll end up a drunkard just like your father.
JOSUÉ: Just like you, you mean! Haven't you anywhere better to go? Why d'you come with me?!

The boy's words seem to affect DORA *deeply.*
DORA: I came to help you. D'you hear that? To help you!
DORA *goes quiet; she seems to have no more arguments at her disposal.*

53. BUS. INT./EXT. DAWN
Sunrise. The bus arrives at a service-station. The driver gets up and speaks to the passengers.
DRIVER: Benemerência stop. Ten minutes.
JOSUÉ *is sleeping with his head leaning on* DORA'S *shoulder. Carefully she moves his head and rests it on the back of the seat. She looks affectionately at the calm face of the sleeping boy. In a sudden gesture, as if she had to do something quickly before she changed her mind, she takes a wad of large notes out of the remaining money. She takes* JOSUÉ'S *wallet out of his knapsack and puts the greater part of the money there. She gets up and goes to the driver.*
DORA: Just a minute, please. It's like this, I'm travelling with my nephew. He's going to meet his father up there in Bom Jesus do Norte. But I'm not going any further on. I'd like to ask you a favour, if you get him to this address.
DORA *gives him a note with the name and address of* JOSUÉ'S *father written on it.*
DRIVER: Look, lady, it's not as easy as that. What if something happens to the child . . .

She shows him some bank notes.
DORA: Hold on for a moment, please. Half a minute. This here is for you. Take it. You can take it. Please.

54. SECOND SERVICE-STATION. INT. DAWN
Detail of a hand holding out some money.
DORA: One ticket to Rio de Janeiro.
WOMAN AT THE TICKET-OFFICE: 60 *reals.*
The ticket-woman gives her a ticket with the change.
DORA *goes to the little bar in the place and sits down opposite the bus platform to have a beer.*

55. SECOND SERVICE-STATION. INT. DAWN
The bus that DORA *came in with the boy leaves. Between two sips of the beer on the table in front of her, she watches it leave. She pays the bill with the last coins left in her wallet. When she turns round, though, she finds* JOSUÉ *sitting at a table in another room. He, as always, pretends not to see her. She goes towards him. A certain shock at seeing him there can't be hidden, however. The two stare at each other for a good while.*
DORA: You shouldn't've done that, boy. You should've gone on in that bus. You were right. It'd have been better for you without me. Everything was fixed. Why don't you want to let go of me now, kid?
He pretends not to hear her.

DORA: When you want to say something, I'm
   over there at the other table.
DORA *goes back to the table she was sitting at. She
looks at* JOSUÉ. *Suddenly, she looks thunderstruck.*
DORA: Where's your knapsack, lad?
He doesn't answer.
DORA (*cont.*) (*shouting*): Where's your knapsack,
   kid?
She goes over to him and grabs him by the shoulders.
DORA: Tell me you didn't leave your knapsack,
   there on the bus!
DORA *runs and tries to see if the bus can still be seen
down the road, which is empty. She only sees the dust
it raises as it goes out of sight. Inconsolable, she gives
up. She sits on the ground and puts her head between
her legs. A deformed goat moves across the yard.*

56. SECOND SERVICE-STATION. INT. DAWN
JOSUÉ *sleeps huddled at a table in a corner. A bus is
blowing gently on its horn.*

   DORA, *sitting on a seat near the boy, comes out of
her state of torpor. Determinedly, she goes over to the
window where she bought the ticket to Rio.*
DORA: Please, I've decided not to go to Rio, I'd
   like to sell the ticket.
TICKET-SELLER: I can't give you the money back
   now, lady. The bus for Rio was that one
   there, that's just gone.
DORA *is forlorn.*

57. SNACK BAR IN THE SERVICE-STATION. INT. MORNING

DORA and JOSUÉ kill time sitting at the counter of the snack bar. JOSUÉ doesn't take his eyes off the food that a man sitting next to him, seemingly one of the truck-drivers parked at the station, is eating. The man sees him looking. DORA nudges the boy. The man smiles at them.

TRUCK-DRIVER: Like some?

The man puts a plate with fried manioc beside them. DORA and JOSUÉ look at one another.

JOSUÉ: No thanks.

DORA: Yes thanks.

TRUCK-DRIVER: I'd be glad if you'd help me out anyway; I'm not hungry any more.

JOSUÉ begins to attack the manioc. Exhausted, DORA wipes her face with her arm.

TRUCK-DRIVER: You don't look a bit well.

DORA: It's my heart. I think it's the palpitations.

TRUCK-DRIVER: Look, press your little finger like this, where the heart beats, it helps . . .

The truck-driver does the gesture and JOSUÉ imitates him. The truck-driver laughs. DORA smiles.

58. THE ROAD. EXT. DAY

The camera passes along a truck, covered with religious sayings like 'Everything is strength, only God is Power'. On the driving-seat are JOSUÉ, DORA and the truck-driver.

59. TRUCK. INT. DAY

The boy looks at the driver, who sees him looking and smiles at him.

TRUCK-DRIVER: Are you going to Bom Jesus to fulfil a promise for the boy?

DORA *thinks it over. She looks at* JOSUÉ.

DORA: You can say that again . . .

JOSUÉ: Where do you live?

TRUCK-DRIVER: I live here.

JOSUÉ: And your wife?

DORA *gives* JOSUÉ *a little pinch.*

DORA: The boy asks everyone that. What's up?

TRUCK-DRIVER: The road's my wife. I've got no family.

JOSUÉ: So you're just like her.

The two look at each other, embarrassed.

60. THIRD SERVICE-STATION (SÃO ROQUE). EXT. AFTERNOON

The driver parks his truck by the station platform. The three get down from the truck.

TRUCK-DRIVER: If you'll excuse me a moment, I've some work to do. It'll be done in twenty minutes.

He goes to the back of the truck and comes out with a sack full of lemons.

DORA: Go and help the man, Josué, go on.

JOSUÉ *and the man go off carrying in the direction of the little store in the bus station.* DORA *goes into the next-door snack bar.*

61. STATION STORE. INT. DAY

The driver puts the sacks down on the counter of the little store. The owner seems pleased to see him.

OWNER: César, my old friend!

CÉSAR: Hi, Bené! Long time no see! Nice to see you! How long is it? Just a sec while I go and get the other one. You can stay here.

JOSUÉ *is hypnotised by a lad of his own age, to his side, stuffing himself with a huge sandwich.* DORA, *at the next counter, is also looking at the people eating in the snack bar.*

62. STATION STORE. INT. DAY

Taking advantage of the owner being engaged chatting to CÉSAR *about the church they both belong to,* JOSUÉ *walks along the shelves and cautiously pushes anything he can reach into his shorts: bread, biscuits, fruit, chocolates. He cunningly escapes.*

63. SNACK BAR. INT. DAY

JOSUÉ *leaves the store and goes over to* DORA *in the snack bar. She immediately sees how full his shorts are.*

DORA: What've you got there?

JOSUÉ: Let's go to the truck and eat it.

DORA: Come here, boy! Put it here, put it here in my bag, go on, now. Go on, I'm going to take it back. Go on, now!

JOSUÉ: Why? Ow, ouch!

JOSUÉ *puts the food in* DORA'S *bag.*
DORA *goes resolutely towards the store.*

64. STORE. INT. DAY.
DORA *goes into the store.* CÉSAR *is still talking to the owner at the counter. Instead of giving the goods back,* DORA *sees her chance, walks along the shelves and herself purloins some yoghurts and a pressed ham. As she goes out,* DORA *passes next to the counter. The child who was eating the sandwich nudges the shop-owner and points at* DORA.
CÉSAR: And every day more brothers join us . . .
SHOP-OWNER: Could you open your bag, please, madam?
DORA *goes pale.*
DORA: What?
SHOP-OWNER: You heard very well! Open your bag this instant!
CÉSAR: Sorry, Bené, I know this lady, she's my friend.
SHOP-OWNER: If you'd open your bag we can clear it all up.
CÉSAR: Bené, for the sake of our friendship, you're even my brother in Christ, I can't let this happen to a lady who's my friend, Dona . . . Joana!
SHOP-OWNER (*not convinced*): If that's the way it is, then OK, César. I must have seen wrong.
CÉSAR: Thanks, Bené.

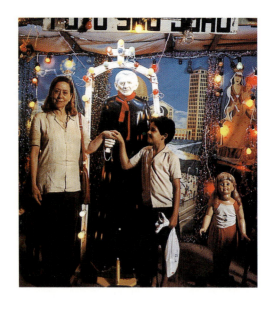

SHOP-OWNER (*ironic*): Well? Wouldn't you like to buy anything?
DORA: There's nothing I'd want to take, thanks very much!
DORA *leaves the shop.*

65. TRUCK. INT. DAY
DORA *gets on to the truck seat and sits down beside* JOSUÉ.
DORA: Never again, don't do that ever again. All you needed to do was ask me. *She opens the bag and begins to take the food out.*
DORA (*cont.*): Look here, how much I bought with the little bit of money I had left. And there's still some left for something else!
JOSUÉ *looks her in the eye.* DORA *is devouring the food.*
DORA: What is it?
JOSUÉ: You didn't have any more money!
DORA: I did have a bit left. Look here, just eat it . . .
JOSUÉ: That's a lie!
DORA: What?
JOSUÉ: You went there, you didn't buy a thing and you even robbed some more!
DORA: Have a bit more respect. Remember I could be your mother!
JOSUÉ: My mother wouldn't have robbed the way you did!

JOSUÉ *starts eating too.*

JOSUÉ: What's more, she didn't drink the way you do!

The two of them face one another.

DORA: That's right! The one who really put the drink away was your father!

JOSUÉ: No. He built the house on his own, he knows how to make anything with wood, OK . . .

DORA: OK. Your father's a drunkard, sonny. A drunkard! Know what that is? A drunkard. Your father's a drunkard.

JOSUÉ: That's a lie! You're ugly and you're a liar! That's why no one's married you! You look like a man, you've not even got make-up! Not like Irene . . .

DORA: Even with all that make-up, she never got married.

They stop talking so they can eat. DORA *makes a sandwich.*

DORA: Always nick boloney!

JOSUÉ: I hate boloney!

CÉSAR *gets up into the truck. He is surprised by how much food the two suddenly have.* DORA *is embarrassed.*

DORA: Would you like some?

CÉSAR: No thanks. I'd like to apologise for what happened there in the shop, Dona . . .

DORA: Dora. Dora. But Joana was fine too . . .

CÉSAR: Dora.
DORA: Like some?
CÉSAR *smiles.*
CÉSAR: Old Bené is a nice guy, but he's very suspicious . . .
DORA: Yes . . .
CÉSAR *starts the motor, and leaves with the truck.*

66. THE ROAD. EXT. DAY
We see the top of the truck with the words 'With God's help I follow my destiny'.

67. TRUCK. INT. DAY
JOSUÉ *is thrilled to be travelling in the truck.*
DORA: This kid wants to be a truck-driver when he grows up.
CÉSAR: Then he's going to have to have a lot of dough. You think it's cheap, having a truck like this?
JOSUÉ: This is only small. I want one of those great big ones.
DORA *and* CÉSAR *think it's funny.*
DORA: Could the lad hold the wheel for a while?
CÉSAR: Come on. Sit here. Careful not to rev it up. Come, that's it. Come on.
CÉSAR *sits the boy in his lap, next to the wheel.*
JOSUÉ *immediately blows the horn.* CÉSAR *and* DORA *laugh.*

68. TRUCK. EXT. DAY

JOSUÉ *is delighted to have his own truck to drive. The landscape gets more and more arid as the truck crosses the south of the State of Bahia.*

69. SERTÃO[3]. EXT. NIGHT

The truck has stopped in the middle of the outback near the road. CÉSAR *and* DORA *are sitting on the ground next to a small fire.* JOSUÉ *has stayed in the truck.*

CÉSAR: Yep, in the Sertão it can be cold too.

JOSUÉ (*off*): Dora!

DORA: Coming! (*Cont.*) Where are you from?

CÉSAR: I'm from Vitória da Conquista. But I left there a long time ago. Since I've been on the road, it seems like I've changed my way of life ten times over. The only bad thing is that you get to know so many people and never see them again. Even you, we've got to know one another and maybe we'll never see each other again.

DORA: We mustn't lose sight of one another again.

JOSUÉ (*from the truck*): Dora! I'm cold!

DORA: Coming!

Resigned, DORA *gets up and goes towards the truck.*

70. TRUCK. INT. MORNING

The first rays of sunshine penetrate the truck's cab and disturb DORA'S *sleep. Outside,* CÉSAR *is finishing shaving.* DORA *looks at him for a long time.*

71. FOURTH SERVICE-STATION (CRUZEIRO DO NORDESTE). EXT. DAY
The truck stops at the service-station. CÉSAR, DORA *and* JOSUÉ *jump out and go towards the restaurant.*

72. RESTAURANT TOILET. INT. DAY
CÉSAR *and* JOSUÉ *are peeing side by side.*
JOSUÉ: In Rio de Janeiro, I had two girlfriends . . .
JOSUÉ *looks straight at* CÉSAR.
JOSUÉ *(cont.)* Did you know that in Rio de Janeiro all the women have sex before they marry? Every single one!
CÉSAR *zips up his flies.*

73. RESTAURANT. INT. DAY
CÉSAR *and* JOSUÉ *come out of the toilet and sit down at a table with* DORA. *A woman from the restaurant comes up.*
WOMAN: What would you like?
DORA: Nothing. We're only here to keep him company.
CÉSAR: Certainly not. I insist on inviting you. (*To the woman*) Bring three meals, and water for me . . . and for you?
DORA: A beer.
WOMAN (*to* CÉSAR) And for your son?
JOSUÉ: A *guaraná*.[4]
CÉSAR: What do you do for a living, Dora?

DORA: I was a primary-school teacher.
JOSUÉ: That's not true! She's a letter-writer. She makes money writing letters for people who don't know how to write.
DORA *looks daggers at* JOSUÉ.
DORA: Well, after I retired I started to do that to help out with the expenses. Don't you like table-soccer? Go and play! Go away and play, kid! Off you go!
JOSUÉ *gets up and goes over to a table-soccer at the back of the room. The woman appears with the drinks.*
DORA *helps herself to beer and fills* CÉSAR's *glass.*
CÉSAR: No, no, no. I can't drink. I'm evangelical.
DORA: I'm quite sure Him up there's not looking.
DORA *fills* CÉSAR's *glass, and he finishes it with a single swig.* DORA *smiles. Her manner, usually sharp, gives way to a gentle tone, a delicate softness one wouldn't expect.*
DORA: I'd like to tell you something . . . I'm very happy I missed that bus . . . very happy.
She fills CÉSAR's *glass again, and he has another swig.*
DORA *looks in* CÉSAR's *eyes and moves closer to him.*
CÉSAR *stops talking and blushes. The woman comes over with* JOSUÉ's *drink; he's playing table-soccer.*
WOMAN: Your *guaraná*.
DORA *holds* CÉSAR's *hands tightly. Dumbfounded, he doesn't know what to do.*

JOSUÉ *interrupts his game and watches the scene from afar.*
DORA: Just a moment, I'll be back in a moment.

74. BATHROOM. INT. DAY
DORA *finishes washing her face and looks at herself in the mirror for a while. A woman comes in and puts red lipstick on. She looks at her attentively.*
DORA: Could you please lend me your lipstick?
WOMAN (*handing it over*): It's right at the end.
You can have it.
DORA: Thanks.
We come closer to DORA *putting on the lipstick. With having lost the habit, she puts it on slowly, a bit awkwardly, with her eyes fixed on the new face reflected in the mirror.*

75. RESTAURANT. INT./EXT. DAY
DORA *comes out of the bathroom. She's happy, and the lipstick suits her. When she goes to the table, however, she finds* CÉSAR *is no longer there.* JOSUÉ *is still at the table-soccer. But there's no sign of anyone else in the restaurant. Through the window,* DORA *sees the truck leaving and starts to cry.*

76. ROAD. EXT. DAY
DORA *and* JOSUÉ *are waiting seated by the side of the road opposite the restaurant, beside a small obelisk in the shape of a lighthouse.*

JOSUÉ: Why did César go away?

DORA *tries to see if any vehicles are coming along the road.*

DORA: You haven't got an answer to that question, kid, have you?

JOSUÉ: He got afraid. He's a queer, isn't he?

DORA: No. No, he's not.

After a while, a truck appears.

JOSUÉ: Can I say something? You look much prettier with lipstick, much prettier.

DORA *tries to hold back the emotion. The truck stops a little before them.* DORA *goes with* JOSUÉ *to the truck to speak to the driver at the window. The ill-tempered man looks her up and down.*

DORA (*to* JOSUÉ): Come here! (*To the driver*) Good afternoon . . .

DRIVER: Good afternoon!

DORA: Are you by any chance going to Bom Jesus?

DRIVER: Yes, ma'am. It's a way off, and I charge 10 a head from here to there.

DORA *takes her watch off and hands it to the driver, who looks it over.*

DORA *and* JOSUÉ *get up into the body of the truck. Under a large canvas, the pilgrims have improvised a real collective home. As the truck leaves, they begin to sing the* 'benditos', *pilgrims' songs.* JOSUÉ *joins in the chorus,* SOTTO VOCE. DORA, *a fish out of water, tries to make herself comfortable in there.*

77. ROAD. EXT. DAY
The truck passes through the scorched landscape. There is no sign of life by the side of the road.

78. PILGRIMS' TRUCK. INT. DAY
JOSUÉ *can't take his eyes off the jerked meat a* PILGRIM *is eating. The man sees the boy's greedy eyes, feels sorry for him and comes over to* DORA *and* JOSUÉ *to offer the food.*
PILGRIM: Have some?
DORA *can't hide her repugnance for the dirty bits of meat.*
DORA: No thanks.
JOSUÉ: Yes thanks.
JOSUÉ *chooses his piece.*
PILGRIM: That's the way, the lad's growing. How old is he?
JOSUÉ: Nine.
PILGRIM: If they'd'a let me, when I was nine, I'd 'a eaten a whole ox. *The pilgrim goes back to his seat.*
JOSUÉ: Eat it, it's good.
DORA: No, I'm far too old to eat that.
JOSUÉ: Just as you like.

79. ROAD. EXT. DAY
The truck enters a track and stops next to a mountain with a little white church on top.

80. HILL. EXT. DAY
Resigned, DORA jumps out of the body of the truck with JOSUÉ. JOSUÉ climbs up the hill to DORA.

81. HILL. EXT. DUSK
DORA and JOSUÉ are sitting on a stone, at a certain distance from the pilgrims, who are singing religious songs. JOSUÉ can't take his eyes off the landscape in front of him.
JOSUÉ: My mother always said that my dad would show me the Sertão one day. (*Pause*) Where must she be now?
DORA doesn't know what to say.
JOSUÉ: D'you think they buried her right?
DORA thinks hard. She takes JOSUÉ's mother's worn handkerchief out of her bag. She gets up and pulls JOSUÉ down the hill.
DORA: This is your mother's; put it there.
JOSUÉ puts the handkerchief on a crucifix amongst the hundreds of ribbons and candles that the pilgrims have deposited there.

82. ROAD. EXT. DUSK
The truck continues along the road.

83. CRUZEIRO DO NORDESTE. EXT. DAY
Bom Jesus do Norte. Trucks full of pilgrims are arriving all the time. Parked just outside the town, the trucks create, overnight, another nomadic town. A labyrinth of

bars, travelling photographers, and one-armed bandits introduces a profane note into the religious festival.

84. STREET. EXT. DAY
DORA pulls JOSUÉ by the hand, forcing her way through the alleys crowded with people, with street-vendors, the loudspeakers pouring out songs and various religious exhortations to complete the hubbub. Both of them are dirty and dishevelled.
JOSUÉ: Are we going to my father's house?
DORA: Yes. Are you happy?
DORA notices that the boy is no longer walking by her side. He's stopped a little behind. She goes over to him.
DORA: What's wrong? You're not telling me you're giving up now?
JOSUÉ looks down, ashamed.
JOSUÉ: I don't want my father to see me this way, all dirty, like a beggar.

85. STREET IN CRUZEIRO DO NORTE. EXT. DAY
DORA begins to tidy JOSUÉ'S hair with a comb borrowed from a vendor's stall. The boy has washed his face, and looks a bit better, in spite of his dirty, crumpled clothes.
DORA: Your father will like you, Josué. Don't worry. It's more whether you like him.
JOSUÉ: I like him.
DORA: Your dad isn't what you think, you know. He's not.
JOSUÉ: You don't know him. He made our house

all on his own, he makes all kinds of things
with wood . . .
DORA: OK, OK! I know, I know, I know! I
know it all by heart, all that. Soon now,
you're going to be there with your father . . .
JOSUÉ: If you want, I can ask him if you could
stay a few days with us . . .
DORA *smiles. She takes the letter out of her pocket and turns round to talk to the owner of the stall.*
DORA: Do you know where this place is?
DORA *shows the letter to the woman.*

86. JESSÉ'S HOUSE. EXT./INT. DUSK
DORA *and* JOSUÉ *walk along a track in the country at the edge of the town. They see a house.* JOSUÉ *runs on ahead. A boy of* JOSUÉ'S *age comes out. He stops running. The two look at one another.*
BOY: Mum, there's a boy here.
DORA *gets to the door of the house and claps her hands to say she's there.*
DORA: Anybody there!?
A very old woman, friendly and part-deaf, is sitting on the sofa in the room.
OLD WOMAN: Yes.
DORA: Good afternoon.
OLD WOMAN: Good afternoon.
DORA: Is this Jesus's house?
OLD WOMAN: Yes it is. Do you want to speak to him?

DORA: Well yes, I'd like to. Is he at home?
OLD WOMAN: No, he's gone out but he'll be back. You can wait if you like.
DORA *comes into the house.*
DORA: Excuse me.
OLD WOMAN: Do come in . . .
A woman with a child comes into the room.
OLD WOMAN: She wants to speak to your husband.
The woman doesn't take her eyes off JOSUÉ, *who's come into the room.*
WOMAN: Have you given her some coffee, Dona Violeta?
DORA: No thanks.
WOMAN: Can you maybe tell me what it is you want to talk to my husband about?
DORA: I have to talk to him. I hope that's all right.
DORA *and* JOSUÉ *sit waiting. A strong wind begins to blow and stops when a middle-aged man enters the house. He has a decent appearance and looks trustworthy. He greets his wife and children.*
WOMAN (*to the man*): Your friends are waiting to talk to you.
The man looks at the two of them, curiously. He suspects something. The woman notices his attitude.
DORA: Good afternoon. I've come from Rio de Janeiro, and I've got a private matter to speak to you about.
MAN (*tense*): All right. Maria, mother, excuse me.

The two women move into the next room, the wife with a suspicious look. The children, on tenterhooks, don't obey the orders to leave, and the man hits them a few times.

MAN (*to the children*): Out, come on, out, outa here!

Finally they obey. JOSUÉ *looks on, horrified. Suspicious, the man examines the boy.*

MAN: Go on, madam.

DORA *looks at* JOSUÉ. *She thinks hard before she breaks into speech.*

DORA: I'm bringing you this boy. His mother's died and now he's only got you in the world.

JOSUÉ *looks, furious, at* DORA, *principally when she says these final words. The man examines* JOSUÉ, *with a serious face. He's tense.*

MAN: And what have you to do with him?

DORA: Nothing.

MAN: Then why did you bring him here?

DORA: I'm a friend of his, you might say . . .

MAN: Is he a good boy?

DORA *looks at* JOSUÉ *and smiles.*

DORA (*smiling at* JOSUÉ): Yes, yes, he is. (*Pause*) This letter is for you.

DORA *hands the man* ANA's *letter. He reads the name written on the envelope and laughs with relief.*

MAN: It's not me, lady. I'm Jessé. This letter is for Jesus, who lived here before . . . Just wait a moment while I fetch something.

The man gets up and leaves the room. DORA *and* JOSUÉ *are in a state of shock. The man soon comes back with a piece of paper in his hand.*

MAN: Here: this is the address he's living at now. It's in Vila do João. He won a house in a raffle and sold this one here. And I'll tell you something, lady, he drank the whole house, down at the bar . . .

JOSUÉ *goes outside alone.*

87. TELEPHONE BOOTH/IRENE'S APARTMENT. INT. DUSK

DORA *is in a phone booth. The phone rings in Irene's apartment.*

(Cuts from one to the other)

IRENE: Hello!

DORA: Irene!

IRENE: Hi, Dora! Everything OK?

DORA: Did you send the money I asked you to?

IRENE *(triumphant)*: The money's waiting for you, there in Bom Jesus da Lapa.

DORA *(incredulous)*: Bom Jesus what?

IRENE: Isn't it Lapa?

DORA *slams the telephone down.*

IRENE: Dear me.

88. STREET. EXT. DUSK

DORA *drags* JOSUÉ *again through the confusion of the street. They go towards the way out of town.*

DORA: I couldn't get a sodding truck to get me out of here away from these damn pilgrims.

JOSUÉ: Where are we going now?

DORA: We're going on foot. See if we can get a lift on the road.

JOSUÉ: On foot?!

DORA: Yes, on foot! Oh God, oh God! I don't know what I did to God to deserve this, I just don't know. You've been sent here to punish me!

JOSUÉ: I'm hungry . . .

DORA: And me! You think I'm not hungry? It's only you that's hungry, not me?! There's no food, there's no money, there's no more food. It's finished. If that's what you want to know, it's finished!

JOSUÉ: What are we going to do now?

DORA (*starting to yell*): I don't know, I don't know! Your father and mother put you in the world, they shouldn't have. Because now it's me here, I've got to put up with it, what a disaster. You're a disaster. You're a disaster.

When she turns round, DORA *sees* JOSUÉ *running back towards where all the pilgrims are.*

DORA: Oh shit! Oh God Almighty! Shit! Josué! Where're you going? Come back, lad! Josué! Come back, kid! Josué! Josué!

She runs after him. She gives her all chasing him, but he's so agile that he gets further and further away until she loses sight of him altogether. Staggering, faint with exhaustion and hunger, she goes on searching for him in the chaos. Hundreds of people are singing hymns, kneeling down, getting up and putting offerings at the feet of the Virgin Mary in the centre of the town square.

DORA *tries to make her way through the people.*
DORA: Josué, Josué!
DORA *just manages to see the child's back slipping away through the crowd.*
DORA: Where've you gone? Josué, Josué, come back here!
Nobody seems to be listening to her.
DORA (*shouting*): Josué! Come back here! I didn't mean to say that!
WOMAN (*praying*): Thank you, thank you, Jesus, I'm asking you, praying to you with all my heart. Jesus, with all my soul, Jesus. Bless my family. Oh Child Jesus, bless your pilgrims.
MAN (*praying*): Forgive me, oh Lord, for I am a sinner. For the blood of Christ, oh Lord. See how hard life is for me . . . the blood in my veins . . . in my body, Our Lord Jesus Christ . . . Protect my mother . . . Bless my family, protect me in the blood of Christ . . . Burn, Lord . . . burn, Lord . . . Why so much sacrifice? Why so much pain?
WOMAN: Long live the Blessed Virgin!

89. SACRISTY/MIRACLE ROOM. INT. NIGHT

Pious praying women, pilgrims and penitents are jammed into the corridor of the sacristy leading to the miracle room, the heart and the final goal of the pilgrimage. Many are singing or praying in murmurs. The atmosphere is one of respect and concentration. In the corners of the room, men and women are saying their rosaries kneeling and facing the wall. Others light candles and then kiss the ground. DORA *again tries to push her way through the people to get closer to the boy, who she thinks she's seen going into the sacristy. The people around her look indignantly at* DORA. *A man puts his finger to his lips, telling her to be quiet. In the end she has to go along with the flow of the people.* DORA *manages to get into the miracle room. The walls are completely covered with photos and mementoes from pilgrims who have been granted their wishes. Thousands of faces in little 3x4 photos, and rag dolls, toys, ribbons, locks of hair, watches and medicine boxes are stuck on top of one another, forming a vast patchwork quilt.*

MAN'S VOICE: Let us scatter the darkness . . .

DORA *searches for* JOSUÉ *through the people crammed in the cubicle. The vision of those thousands of faces in the photos on the wall seems to confuse her even more. Things start whirling round her. They all look at* DORA.

PILGRIM WOMAN: Be quiet!

DORA *falls rigid on the ground.* JOSUÉ *appears and kneels down beside her.*

90. BOM JESUS MAIN SQUARE. EXT. DAWN
Very early in the morning, DORA *wakes up with her head in* JOSUÉ'S *lap. The two of them are sitting in the main square of Bom Jesus.*

91. BOM JESUS MAIN SQUARE. EXT. DAY
DORA *and* JOSUÉ *are sitting on the edge of the pavement, in the square which is the heart of the pilgrimage. The activity is beginning. In a nearby stall, pilgrims are having their photos taken with Padre Cícero[5], as offerings to the saint. In another, someone is selling confessions. On the ground pedlars are selling clay ex votos.*

PREACHER: This wicked commerce, this madman's festival, it's the Devil's feast, the den of thieves, Satan's carnival. He's there, down there, he's happy, he's dancing, the Evil One is laughing out loud.

DORA *and* JOSUÉ *play at throwing stones into an old tin can. The camera focuses on a lad playing a guitar and singing. Two* GYPSY WOMEN *pass by.*

GYPSY WOMAN: D'you want know your fortune, lady? 1 *real*.

DORA: I've no money left.

GYPSY WOMAN: Only a little thing! Be so good . . .

DORA: I told you, I've no money left!

GYPSY WOMAN: Be so good . . .
DORA: Stop pestering me!
The GYPSIES go in search of other customers. JOSUÉ looks round. At the photo stall, there are lots of people. He gets up and goes over to it.
DORA: Josué, where're you off to?
JOSUÉ observes the crowds of people buying things. In an imitation studio set up in the stall, a family is posing for a photo, in front of the image of Padre Cícero.
GIRL: How much is it for a portrait with Padre Cícero?
STALL-OWNER: It costs 3 *reals*, lady.
DORA goes over to JOSUÉ.
GIRL: 3 *reals*. As much as that?
STALL-OWNER: 3 *reals*. That's the price.
GIRL: Is that for the photo and the message to the saint?
STALL-OWNER: No, no. It's only for the photo of you and our beloved Padre. Sure you don't want it, lady?
The GIRL moves away from the STALL-HOLDER. DORA puts her hand on JOSUÉ's shoulder, paying no attention to what the stall-holder and the girl are saying.
DORA: Josué, what are we doing by this stall? Come on, let's go.
Suddenly, JOSUÉ goes over to the girl.
JOSUÉ (*to the girl*): Hey, lady. She's a writer. She'll send the saint's message for you.
GIRL: And do you write?

DORA *takes a pen out of her bag to do the girl a good deed.*
JOSUÉ: It's only 1 *real*.

92. STREET. EXT. DAY

DORA *and* JOSUÉ *are already sitting at a table amongst the other stalls in the square. He does the advertising.*
JOSUÉ: Over here for letters! Anyone want to send a letter home, or a message to the saint! Letters here! Only 1 *real*! Letters! Anyone want to send a letter home, or a message to the saint, only 1 *real*!

When DORA *is finishing writing, a* PILGRIM *comes up.*
PILGRIM: I'd like to send a little note, how much does it cost?
JOSUÉ: It's 1 *real*.
PILGRIM: 1 *real*?
JOSUÉ: And 2 if you want us to mail it.
PILGRIM: That's what I want.
JOSUÉ: You can wait in line.
DORA *looks at the boy amazed. The* PILGRIM *counts the money.*
JOSUÉ: Over here for letters! Who wants to send a letter home? Message to the saint!
PILGRIM: OK then. Can I start?
DORA: Go ahead.
PILGRIM: Criselda, my lovely Criselda, I've come from Itabaiana . . .
DORA: Itabaiana . . .
PILGRIM: . . . all the way here, on foot . . .

DORA'S *hand goes on scribbling on the paper. A woman in a bridal dress appears.*
BRIDE: I'm here in Bom Jesus to thank you for the promise I made if Benício'd marry me . . .
A woman in her early thirties appears, carrying an ex-voto, a little wooden bottle.
WOMAN: Thank you, Child Jesus, for the mercy received when my husband left off drinking . . .
Voices and faces appear one after the other.
MAN: Leontina Emerentina . . . Now I can be the happiest man in the world.
DORA: And how long is it since he's been away?
SECOND MAN: It's four years since he left.
DORA: And you've had no news, is that it?
SECOND MAN: No, nothing.
GIRL: Greetings to my mother, Maria Adalgiza Bezerra.
THIRD MAN: Josefa Maria da Silva, there in São Bento do Una.
GIRL: . . . to my fiancé, João Pedro da Silva, there in São Paulo.
CHILDREN: To my father, José Alves da Silva . . .
The voices are superimposed on one another, in an overall buzz.

93. STREET. EXT. NIGHT
Another peasant is dictating. There's no one left in the queue. The activity in the square has also lessened with nightfall.

PEASANT: Thank you, Child Jesus, for the favour received, for having made it rain this year on the farm. I've come to Bom Jesus and set off ten coloured rockets in homage to you. Sebastiano.

DORA *gives the letter to the peasant, who hands her the money.*

PEASANT: Here, lady.

DORA: Your letter . . .

The man goes. JOSUÉ *is counting his treasure over again.*

DORA: We're rich!

JOSUÉ: We can even get something to eat!

94. STREET. EXT. DUSK

Triumphant, DORA *and* JOSUÉ *pose for the photographer of the miracles stall, with the image of Padre Cícero behind them.*

DORA: Come here, Josué.

They stop in front of the stall that sells clothes.

DORA: Let's go, come on! Let's go!

JOSUÉ: I'm going to give you this dress for a present.

DORA: For me?

JOSUÉ: For you!

DORA: Good Lord!

JOSUÉ: How much is it?

STALL-HOLDER: 5 *reals*.

JOSUÉ *buys the dress. They leave.*

JOSUÉ: You'll be a lot prettier with this dress.

95. STREET. EXT. NIGHT
The façade of a run-down hotel.

96. HOTEL ROOM. INT. NIGHT
DORA, *completely exhausted, lies down on the bed.*
DORA: I'm done in.
JOSUÉ *shuts the door behind him, sits down on a chair and empties the bag full of letters into the rubbish bin.*
DORA *finally notices what he's doing.*
DORA: No, don't do that!
JOSUÉ: Don't we have to tear them up first?
DORA *is shocked at the boy's attitude.*
DORA: No. Give them here. I'll think about what to do after, OK?

97. HOTEL ROOM. INT. NIGHT
JOSUÉ *is in the bathroom, with the door half-open.*
DORA *is changing.*
JOSUÉ (*off*): Are we going to look for my father tomorrow?
DORA: Yes. There's a bus at lunchtime.
DORA, *in a slip, gets under the sheets.*
DORA: You can come, Josué. Come on.
JOSUÉ, *in his undergarments, lies down on the bed beside* DORA *and sees her underclothes. She puts out the light.*
DORA: Lie down here. That's it. Good-night, Josué.
JOSUÉ: Good-night, Dora.

DORA *turns over to go to sleep.*

JOSUÉ: Do you always sleep that way?

DORA: How do you want me to sleep? In the buff?

JOSUÉ: Sleeping in the buff's better.

DORA: If you want to take your clothes off, it doesn't bother me, OK?

JOSUÉ *takes no initiative.*

DORA: What's the matter? Feeling shy?

JOSUÉ *looks bashful.*

DORA: I bet you've never seen a woman in the buff.

JOSUÉ: I've already seen loads, OK?

DORA: Oh yeah, your mother!

JOSUÉ: That's a lie, I've seen lots of other women too!

DORA: Only seen, kid? Didn't you do anything else?!

JOSUÉ: I had sex with them!

DORA (*amused*): Had sex? And how did you do that?

JOSUÉ *thinks hard before answering.*

JOSUÉ: It's not a subject you can talk to a woman about.

DORA (*laughing*): How about that! There's a real man in my bed!

DORA *gives* JOSUÉ *an affectionate hug. Frightened, he tries to push her away.*

98. STREET. EXT. DAY
DORA and JOSUÉ are in the street again, sitting on a bench with their backs to a bus stop, where there is a sign with the words 'Viação Estrela do Norte' (Star of the North Transport) on it. JOSUÉ says something, but DORA doesn't hear him. Her mind is somewhere else, her eyes fixed on the little post office in front of her.

99. BUS. EXT. DAY
JOSUÉ: Dora, the bus!
DORA and JOSUÉ get into a bus that's so rickety and jammed with people, it looks as if it's going to fall apart. DORA hardly notices.

100. BUS. INT. DAY
The two end up travelling standing up, squeezed between other passengers carrying enormous bags and even chickens.
JOSUÉ: Full, isn't it?

101. VILA DO JOÃO. EXT. DAY
DORA and JOSUÉ get off with an older couple in Vila do João . . . DORA speaks to the ticket-seller of the bus company.
DORA: F Street, please?
The ticket-seller gets up and calls a young man who's mending the roof of one of the houses.
TICKET-SELLER: Hey, hey there! Whereabouts is F Street?

YOUNG MAN: F is the new street. The one that's been paved. It's down there.
DORA: Thanks.

The two walk on. They go down the main street, A Street. The two hundred prefabricated houses, all the same, look like toy houses, and give the impression of something set up in the middle of nowhere. The two walk quite slowly, as if they're in no hurry to get anywhere.

JOSUÉ: It's all the same, isn't it?
DORA: Yes, all the same.

They walk on.

DORA: Did your mother have a photo of your father?
JOSUÉ: Yes.
DORA: D'you think you can remember your father's face by the photo?
JOSUÉ: There are times when I can. Then it falls to pieces in my head.
DORA: Sometimes I forget my father's face too. We shouldn't have the sodding photographs, so's not to have to remember. They might let people forget! (*She's sorry for what she's said*) I left home when I was sixteen. I never saw my father again. Years later, in the middle of Rio, I came face to face with him. I froze. Then I got my courage up and went to speak to him. 'D'you recognise me? You remember? Remember me?' I saw in his face that he

didn't recognise me, didn't recognise his own daughter. 'Hey, girl, come here. How could I forget a pretty little thing like you . . . ?' I told the old goat I'd got the wrong person and got out of there. I heard he died a bit later. (*She turns to* JOSUÉ) D'you see?

DORA *looks intensely at the boy. He sees how sad she is.*

JOSUÉ: What have I done?

DORA: In a short while you'll have forgotten me too.

He looks at her, puzzled.

JOSUÉ: I don't want to forget you.

DORA: It's no good, you'll forget me.

DORA *and* JOSUÉ *get to F Street.* DORA *checks the number '34' written on the scrap of paper and easily finds the house. The windows and doors are shut, and the general air of abandonment suggests that the house must be unoccupied.* DORA *seems excited by this. She claps her hands to announce her presence.*

DORA (*shouting*): Hey! Jesus!

Still nothing. A man appears at the window of the next-door house.

MAN: Jesus doesn't live here any more, lady.

DORA *goes up to him. A youth comes from behind the man and observes the scene.*

DORA: And you don't know where he lives now?

MAN: No idea. That guy just vanished. Nobody here ever heard of him again.

DORA: Thanks.

The boy who was inside the house gets on a bicycle and goes off in the other direction. The two begin to retrace their steps in silence. They are the only people walking along the street in the midday sun. DORA *looks at* JOSUÉ. *He's more and more depressed. She, on the other hand, seems to be reinvigorated.*

JOSUÉ *looks her in the eye.*

JOSUÉ: And he really isn't coming back?

DORA: No . . . I don't think so.

JOSUÉ: I'm going to wait for him.

DORA (*gently*): It's no good, Josué, he won't come back. (*Pause*) Wouldn't you like to come with me? Hey, kid, I'd like that. You know, don't you? I'd really like that a lot.

JOSUÉ *squeezes her hand, in agreement.*

DORA: Let's go.

102/103. IRENE'S APARTMENT/VILA DO JOÃO. INT. DAY

DORA: The father's disappeared.

IRENE: And now what're you going to do?

DORA: I can't leave the boy here on his own . . .

IRENE: No, you can't . . .

DORA: He really is a good lad, Irene, you know . . .

IRENE (*excited*): Are you going to bring him back home? . . .

DORA: I don't know, I can't make up my mind.
IRENE: What d'you mean, you don't know?
DORA: I've made a lot of mistakes in life, Irene. You know about that.
IRENE: And what're you going to do now, love?
DORA: Listen, Irene. Sell the fridge, sell the sofa. What else have I got?
IRENE: The TV?
DORA: Yes, sell the TV.
IRENE: And now, what're you going to do?
DORA: When I stop somewhere, I'll phone you.

104. VILA DO JOÃO. EXT. DAY
DORA *puts the phone down and goes to the small house to the side, where the bus company operates from. She goes to the ticket-office window. The ticket-clerk is chatting to a man mending the wiring. The man examines the two.*
DORA: I want two tickets back to Bom Jesus.
TICKET-CLERK: The next bus to Bom Jesus is only tomorrow morning.
DORA: And to some other place?
TICKET-CLERK: There's no buses to anywhere else. Only tomorrow too. This is the back of beyond, lady . . .
DORA: What can I do to get out of here?
TICKET-CLERK: Only tomorrow.
The man who was mending the roof appears together with the boy who was in Jesus's house and went off on

a bicycle; he gets up and goes towards DORA *and* JOSUÉ.

MAN: Lady, were you by any chance looking for my father?

JOSUÉ *gets a shock.*

DORA (*uneasy*): Your father?

MAN: Jesus. They've told me there were people who'd come looking for him.

JOSUÉ *grips* DORA'S *arm.*

DORA (*reticent*) Yes . . . that's me.

MAN: Do you know my father?

DORA: Yes, I'm a friend of his. What a coincidence to meet his son.

JOSUÉ *examines* ISAÍAS.

MAN: Not so much of a coincidence as you think, if you look at the size of this place. Pleased to meet you: my name's Isaías.

DORA: It's a pleasure, Isaías. Mine's Dora.

ISAÍAS: So have you come for a visit?

DORA (*she looks at* JOSUÉ): No. I was wandering around, getting to know the area, and I thought I'd go and visit an old friend.

JOSUÉ *pulls at* DORA'S *skirt.*

ISAÍAS: Then I insist you come and have a snack at home. It's not every day someone comes to visit Dad.

DORA: The thing is . . .

ISAÍAS: I insist. You wouldn't snub me that way . . .

DORA *looks at* JOSUÉ.
DORA: No, but the thing is . . .
ISAÍAS: And this is . . . what's your name?
DORA *and* JOSUÉ *look at one another, in a state of shock at the question.*
JOSUÉ: Geraldo.
ISAÍAS: Geraldo, Dona Dora, I insist, I insist, come with me.

105. ISAÍAS'S HOUSE. EXT./INT. AFTERNOON
DORA, JOSUÉ *and* ISAÍAS *chat as they walk towards a house which is better maintained than those around it.*
ISAÍAS: Geraldo, come here. Come over here. D'you know tongue-twisters?
JOSUÉ: No.
ISAÍAS: Peter Piper picked a peck of pickled pepper. A peck of pickled pepper Peter Piper picked.
JOSUÉ: Peter Piper picked a pick of peckled papper . . .
ISAÍAS: You're really dumb!
They come up to the front door.
ISAÍAS: This is the house that me and my brother Moisés came to live in after Dad went away. Hey, Moisés! We've got visitors!
They go into the house. Inside, everything is impeccably tidy. MOISÉS *comes from inside and joins them. He is about seventeen and has a childlike smile.*

ISAÍAS: Moisés, this is Dona Dora, a friend of
   Dad's. What a thing, eh?
DORA: Pleased to meet you.
Suddenly, MOISÉS *stops smiling and goes expressionless.*
MOISÉS: Pleased to meet you.

106. MOISÉS'S WORKSHOP. INT. DAY
The four of them go into a small house at the bottom of the yard. On the way out, on the wall, JOSUÉ *sees two enamelled portraits, which almost look like paintings. We easily recognise* ANA, JOSUÉ'S *mother. The face by her side is evidently that of Jesus. His face suggests an unsuspected innocence. In the photos, the two of them, sure of themselves, have possibly just been married.*
ISAÍAS *puts the light on revealing a complete carpentry workshop.*
ISAÍAS: All this is land we invaded[6], Dona Dora.
   We invaded everything. We grabbed this
   house after Father lost the other one. Then
   we set up this carpentry shop here. Moisés
   chisels away here all day. He's working even
   better than Father. *Inquisitive,* JOSUÉ *examines the wood and the tools.*
ISAÍAS: He makes tables, he makes chairs, he
   makes everything. We're even selling things in
   the State capital!
MOISÉS *turns the mechanical lathe on, picks up a file and begins to mould a piece of wood.* JOSUÉ *is*

astonished to see coming out of the wood a spinning top just like his own. MOISÉS *notices how the boy is fascinated by his work.*

ISAÍAS: Hey, Geraldo, come on over here.

JOSUÉ *comes close to the lathe.* MOISÉS *helps him operate the lathe. To* ISAÍAS'S *and* MOISÉS'S *astonishment, the lad works the machine with surprising skill.* DORA *watches the scene attentively.*

107. THE DOOR OF ISAÍAS'S HOUSE. EXT. DAY

ISAÍAS, MOISÉS *and* JOSUÉ *stop playing football in the middle of the street and come over to join* DORA, *who was watching them, sitting on the steps of the entrance to the house.* JOSUÉ *straightaway comes and sits beside her.*

MOISÉS: The youngster really knows how to play football!

DORA: Don't sing his praises, he's too full of himself as it is.

JOSUÉ (*to* DORA): I'm not too bad, it's them that are lousy.

DORA *laughs.*

108. ISAÍAS'S HOUSE. INT. DUSK

DORA *is sitting in the living-room with* JOSUÉ, ISAÍAS, *and* MOISÉS. *They are drinking coffee in silence.* MOISÉS *is standing in the doorway.*

ISAÍAS: Give it her, give it so she can read it to us.

MOISÉS: Forget it, Isaías. What's she got to do with this?!

ISAÍAS: She's a friend of Dad's. We can trust her, Moisés. Please give it her. *There's a silence.*

ISAÍAS *(cont.)*: Then I'll go and get it.

MOISÉS: Then you're going to hunt for that wretch.

ISAÍAS *gets up, and goes to the chest, opens a drawer and takes out the blue envelope of a letter.*

ISAÍAS: This letter came here six months ago, from Father to Ana Fontenele, a woman he was with after our late mother died. Ana Fontenele went to Rio de Janeiro about . . . nine years ago, with our younger brother in her womb.

MOISÉS: Father waited about two years for Ana Fontenele to come back from Rio de Janeiro. He stopped working and he drank, drank, drank. Then he had to sell the house in Bom Jesus to pay his debts.

MOISÉS *doesn't take his eyes off* JOSUÉ.

ISAÍAS: Then, one day I got up and Dad was no longer in the house. There was a half-full bottle of *cachaça*[7] on the table. Then I thought: for my dad to leave a bottle of *cachaça* half-full, something pretty bad must have happened.

MOISÉS: He vanished. It was better for us. Only that way we managed to get some

money together and make things better for
ourselves.
ISAÍAS: Don't talk that way, Moisés!
MOISÉS: It's the truth, and it's got to be said!
ISAÍAS *turns to* DORA.
ISAÍAS: You know our father, you know he's a
good guy . . .
MOISÉS: Some good guy . . .
ISAÍAS: I'm going to give it her to read.
JOSUÉ *finally emerges from his silence.*
JOSUÉ (*to* MOISÉS): Give it her to read.
ISAÍAS *and* MOISÉS *are surprised at the boy's reaction
and exchange glances.*
MOISÉS: But the letter is for Ana, not for us. You
know Father never had any time for us.
ISAÍAS: But Ana Fontenele never came back. So
we'd better open it, Moisés. (*To* DORA)
Would it be too much trouble for you to read
it to us?
DORA: Of course not.
MOISÉS *gives* DORA *the letter. She looks at it
closely. The three of them look on anxiously as
she cautiously opens the envelope and takes out
the letter inside.* DORA *begins reading just for herself.
She gets a shock. Her audience's curiosity mounts
further.*
MOISÉS: Well?
ISAÍAS: Does it say where he is?
JOSUÉ: Come on, read it.

DORA *looks at the three of them. She summons her courage before she reads.*

DORA (*reading*): 'Ana, you wretch, with a great deal of effort I managed to find a writer to tell you only now I've cottoned you must've gone back and found our new house while I'm here in Rio de Janeiro looking for you. I want to get there before this letter but if it gets there before me, listen to what I've got to say to you: wait for me. I'm coming back home too.'

MOISÉS: It's six months since that letter got here.

DORA: It must be because he's not managed to get back. (*She goes on reading*) 'I left Moisés and Isaías looking after things.'

MOISÉS: Left us to look after things, that's a good one.

DORA (*goes on reading*): 'Ana, I'm thinking I might spend another month at the mine[8] before I go back home. But wait for me because I'll come back. And then we'll all be together, me, you, Isaías, Moisés . . . (*Pause*) and Josué . . . and Josué who I want so much to know. You're a stubborn little woman, but I'd give everything I've got just to look at you again. Forgive me. It's me and you together in this life. Jesus.'

ISAÍAS: He's going to come back.

MOISÉS: He'll never be back!

JOSUÉ (*finally giving his opinion*): One day he'll be back.

They are all impressed with the boy's confident

prophecy. ISAÍAS *is visibly disturbed. He can't keep his eyes off* JOSUÉ.

109. JESUS'S HOUSE EXT. NIGHT
DORA *finds* JOSUÉ *sitting on the pavement in front of the house, looking at the sky.*
JOSUÉ: Dora, did my father really put in the letter that he wanted to know me?
DORA: Course he did.
JOSUÉ: He didn't, I know he didn't.
DORA *tries to find something to say when* ISAÍAS *comes out of the house calling for them.*
ISAÍAS: Hey, folks! Come on in. I prepared Father's room for you, OK, Dona Dora?
DORA: Thanks.
ISAÍAS: Come on, lad, a tongue-twister.
JOSUÉ: Again?
ISAÍAS: She sells sea shells by the sea shore . . . Go on . . .
JOSUÉ: She sells, she sells . . .
ISAÍAS: You really are dumb!

110/111. ROOM INT. DAWN
DORA *gets up without making any noise and slowly opens the door. From her angle, we see in the other room the three brothers sleeping together, protecting each other. Putting on the cheerful cheap cotton dress that* JOSUÉ *bought for her at the pilgrim stall,* DORA *puts on the lipstick that the boy said looked good on her.*

112. ISAÍAS'S HOUSE. INT. EARLY MORNING
DORA *looks again at the sleeping boy. She pulls herself together. Before she goes out, she stops in front of the chest in the living-room, below the portrait* JOSUÉ *looked at earlier. On it is Jesus's letter.* DORA *takes* ANA'S *letter out of her bag, putting it on top of the other. She stands stock still for a moment, and then finally makes up her mind and goes through the doorway.*

113. VILA DO JOÃO. EXT. EARLY MORNING
DORA *walks quickly towards the entrance to the town.*

114. ISAÍAS'S HOUSE. INT. EARLY MORNING
JOSUÉ *wakes up and looks round the house for* DORA.
JOSUÉ: Dora!

115. VILA DO JOÃO. EXT. EARLY MORNING
A decrepit bus comes to the stop in Vila do João. DORA *gets on it.*

116. VILA DO JOÃO. EXT. EARLY MORNING
JOSUÉ *comes out of the house and goes into the middle of the street. He knows something's happened and begins to run.*

117. BUS. INT. EARLY MORNING
The bus leaves Vila do João. The landscape seen through the side windows is blurred by the speed of the

bus. We come close to DORA'S *face. Her eyes are brimming, and it's an effort to hold back the tears. She finally makes up her mind, opens her bag, takes out her old block of letter-paper and a pen.*

118. VARIOUS. MORNING
We alternate between DORA *and* JOSUÉ.
A detail of a hand writing on letter-paper.
DORA (*off*): 'Josué, it's a long time since I've written a letter to anyone. Now, I'm sending this one to you . . .'
JOSUÉ *gets to the bus stop breathless, but there are no longer any signs of the bus.*
DORA *writes the letter sitting on the bus seat. Detail of her hand scribbling on paper.*
DORA (*off*) (*cont.*): 'You're right. Your father will come back one day, and I'm sure he's everything you think he is.'
JOSUÉ, *upset, sits on the edge of the pavement next to the bus stop.* DORA *goes on writing the letter to* JOSUÉ.
DORA (*off*) (cont.): I remember my father taking me to the locomotive he drove. I was only a little girl and he let me blow the train's whistle all the way along the line. When you're driving along the roads in your big truck, I want you to remember that I was the first person who got you to put your hands on the wheel.

As if moved by intuition, JOSUÉ *gets up and looks along the road.*

DORA (*off*) (*cont.*): It'll be better too for you to stay there with your brothers. You deserve more than I can give you. Whenever you want to remember me, take a look at the photo we had taken together.

At the bus stop. JOSUÉ *looks at the empty road.*

DORA (*off*) (*cont.*): I say that because I'm afraid you might forget me one day too. (*Pause*) I miss my father. I miss everything . . . Dora.

DORA *stops writing and looks out. She is silently crying. She takes a little viewer with the photo that she had taken with* JOSUÉ *in the miracle-stall.* DORA *looks affectionately at the photo, in which she and* JOSUÉ *look happy, with the image of Padre Cícero in the background.* JOSUÉ, *at the bus stop, does the same.* DORA *dries her tears with her hands.* JOSUÉ *is smiling. The camera focuses on* DORA's *face. She is weeping and smiling at the same time.*

NOTES

1. The North-East of Brazil, comprising some ten states and containing a third of Brazil's population, is also the poorest area in the country, and the one which provides the largest number of emigrants to the industrialized South, above all to Rio de Janeiro and São Paulo. The marked accent of the area has a sing-song intonation.

2. A *real*: the present currency of Brazil. At the time of the action, one *real* was worth slightly less than one dollar.

3. The Sertão: a contraction of the Portuguese word for a large desert (*desertão*), this area covers a large part of the interior of the North-East of Brazil. It is subject to periodic droughts, a major cause of emigration.

4. *Guaraná*: a fizzy soft drink, made from an Amazonian plant, and very popular throughout Brazil.

5. Padre Cícero: Padre Cícero Romão Batista (1844–1934). A priest in Juazeiro, Ceará, he remains perhaps the most revered religious figure in the interior of the North-East of Brazil. A

controversial man, also involved in politics, he was suspended from religious orders in 1897, but this had no effect on his huge influence on the people of the region, who traditionally call him *'meu padim Ciço'* (my little father Cícero).

6. Invaded: Isaías is saying that the land was taken over, probably by people linked to the Movimento dos Sem-terra (the Landless Movement), as land which was not being properly used, and was needed by the poor.

7. *Cachaça*: a strong, and very cheap alcoholic drink made from sugar-cane.

8. Mine (*garimpo*): this implies that Jesus is (or says he is) working in the gold-prospecting areas which in the eighties and nineties attracted large numbers of poor labourers to places such as Serra Pelada, in the Amazon area. They have reached international notoriety in part through the photographs of Sebastião Salgado.

CREDITS

Director: Walter Salles

Producer: Elisa Tolomelli

Director of Photography: Walter Carvalho

Screenplay: João Emanuel Carneiro and Marcos Bernstein

(Based on an original idea by Walter Salles)

Artistic Direction: Cassio Amarante and Carla Caffé

Wardrobe: Cristina Camargo

Sound: Jean-Claude Brisson

Soundtrack: Antônio Pinto and Jaques Morelenbaum

Directors of Production: Marcelo Torres and Afonso Coaracy

Coordinator of Production: Beto Bruno

Front Production: Selma Santos

Set Manager: Leonardo Oest

Make-up: Antoine Garabedian

Props: Mônica Costa

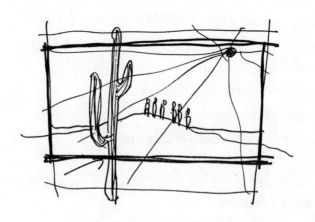

CAST

Dora	Fernanda Montenegro
Irene	Marília Pêra
Josué	Vinicius de Oliveira
Ana	Sôia Lira
Isaías	Matheus Nachtergaele
César	Othon Bastos
Pedrão	Otávio Augusto
Moisés	Caio Junqueira
Yolanda	Stela Freitas